D0603256

Ludwig II and his Dream Castles

The Fantasy World of a Storybook King

Ludwig Merkle

Bruckmann

Title page: King Ludwig II in general's uniform and coronation robe (excerpt) with Neuschwanstein Castle (top), Linderhof (middle) and Herrenchiemsee (bottom).

Inside front cover: Versailles in Upper Bavaria. Ludwig's Herrenchiemsee Palace.

Inside back cover: Linderhof Castle in the Graswang Valley.

Page 1: King Ludwig II in Bavarian general's uniform.

Pages 2/3: The church of St. Koloman by J. Schmuzer. Neuschwanstein Castle in the background.

Pages 4/5: Fraueninsel in the Chiemsee, with a view of the Chiemgauer Alps.

Pages 6/7: Evening at Neuschwanstein. Below in the valley is Hohenschwangau Castle.

Pages 8/9: The Minstrels' Hall in Neuschwanstein, modelled on a hall in Wartburg Castle.

Pages 10/11: View from Ilkahöhe down to Lake Starnberg and the mountains beyond.

Thèmes titres: Le roi Louis II en uniforme de général et manteau de sacre (détail) avec les châteaux de Neuschwanstein (en haut), Linderhof (au centre), Herrenchiemsee (en bas).

Première page de garde: Versailles en Haute-Bavière. Le château Herrenchiemsee de Louis.

Dernière page de garde: Le château Linderhof dans la vallée du Graswang.

Page 1: Le roi Louis II en uniforme de général bavarois.

Page 2/3: L'église Saint Koloman de J.Schmuzer. Neuschwanstein en arrière-plan.

Page 4/5: La Fraueninsel sur le Chiemsee avec vue sur les Alpes de Chiemgau.

Page 6/7: Neuschwanstein le soir. En bas dans la vallée, le château de Hohenschwangau.

Page 8/9: D'après le modèle du Wartburg: la Salle des Chanteurs de Neuschwanstein.

Page 10/11: Vue des cimes de l'Ilka sur le lac de Starnberg et la chaîne des Alpes.

Soggetti: Re Ludwig II° in uniforme da generale e col manto dell'incoronazione (dettaglio) con i castelli di Neuschwanstein (in alto), di Linderhof (al centro) e di Herrenchiemsee (in basso).

Prima di copertina: La Versailles dell'Alta Baviera. Il castello di Ludwig di Herrenchiemsee.

Ultima di copertina: Il castello di Linderhof nella valle di Graswang.

Pagina 1: Re Ludwig II° in uniforme da generale bavarese.

Pagg. 2/3: Chiesa di St.-Koloman di J. Schmuzer. Sullo sfondo Neuschwanstein.

Pagg. 4/5: La Fraueninsel dello Chiemsee con vista sulle Alpi della Chiemgau.

Pagg. 6/7: Neuschwanstein di sera. In basso, nella valle, il Castello di Hohenschwangau.

Pagg. 8/9: Sul modello della Wartburg: la sala dei cantori a Neuschwanstein.

Pagg. 10/11: Vista dalla Ilkahöhe sul lago Starnberg e la catena alpina.

タイトル：将軍の制服と即位式のコートを着たルートヴィヒII世（部分図）
ノイシュヴァンシュタイン城（上）
リンダーホーフ城（中）
王城ヘレンキームゼー（下）

初めの見開：オーバーバイエルンのヴェルサイユ。ヘレンキームゼーのルートヴィヒ城。

終りの見開：グラスヴァングタールのリンダーホーフ城。

1ページ：バイエルンの将軍の制服を着た国王ルートヴィヒU世。

2/3ページ：Ｊ．シュムツァーの聖コロマン教会。背景にノイシュヴァンシュタイン城。

4/5ページ：キームガウアルプスの眺めとキームゼーのフラウエン島。

6/7ページ：夕刻のノイシュヴァンシュタイン城。谷間にはホーエンシュヴァンガウ城。

8/9ページ：ヴァルトブルク城を模範としたノイシュヴァンシュタイン城の歌人の広間。

10/11ページ:シュタルベルガー湖のイルカヘーエからの眺めとアルプスの連峰。

English translation: Ingrid Taylor, Munich

Translation of the French, Italian and Japanese picture captions: inlingua®, Munich

2nd edition 1996

Printed on paper treated with low-chlorine bleach.

Die Deutsche Bibliothek - CIP data

Merkle, Ludwig: Ludwig II and his dream castles : the fantasy world of a storybook king / Ludwig Merkle. – München : Bruckmann, 1995
Dt. Ausg. u. d. T.: Merkle, Ludwig: Ludwig II. und seine Schlösser
ISBN 3-7654-2769-1
NE: HST

© 1995 F. Bruckmann KG, Munich
All rights reserved
Published by Bruckmann, Munich
Printed in Germany by
Gerber + Bruckmann, Munich
ISBN 3-7654-2769-1

Contents

Foreword

OH, LUDWIG, BAVARIA'S PRIDE

Oh, Ludwig – which other people ever had a more wonderful, more splendid monarch?

He was beautiful, at least in the early days of his reign. After his accession to the throne in 1864 at the age of 18½, he was far and wide the most handsome king. Slender, supple and standing over six feet tall he was a "veritable picture of youthful charm and beauty", in the words of his contemporaries; proud majesty and noble sovereignty radiated from his countenance and his whole bearing; he wore his luxuriant, dark brown hair artistically coiffured in curls and, richly perfumed, he exuded sweet odours wherever he went. All those who saw him were entranced by his unusually expressive face and his large rapturous, dreamy eyes, the colour of which was evidently beyond definition. Some sources claimed they were black, others brown or a deep dark blue; yet others tell of his steely grey or even bright blue eyes.

More reliable information is available on the royal voice. "Full and round in tone", it sounded soft and quiet, "very pleasant" and sonorous, and the King spoke a "pure, unaffected German" (and also very passable French). He could only speak a little Bavarian dialect, and forbade his servants "to speak old Bavarian"; however, he did master enough of it to be able to curse his stable hands, servants and ministry officials when the occasion arose.

The Bavarian people immediately fell in love with their King and began to worship him – Bavarians are known for their loyalty and devotion. Their feelings remained unchanged even when he grew ever more bloated and toothless, a change which took place in a rather short space of time. The poet Felix Dahn who met him in 1864 and then again in 1873 noted: "In the intervening nine years much has disappeared of the youthful beauty which he used to radiate. He has become too fat and his wan facial colour is not attractive, and several missing front teeth spoil his appearance when he speaks..." In 1871, when King Ludwig was 25 years old, Friedrich Wilhelm, Crown Prince of Prussia, also commented on this sad development: "His beauty has much diminished, he has lost his front teeth and looks most pale..."

Ludwig II in 1866 at the age of 21. No wonder the Bavarian people loved this handsome young man.

Louis II, en 1866, à l'âge de 21 ans. Un jeune homme de belle prestance; il n'est pas étonnant qu'il plaisait tant à son peuple.

Ludwig II nel 1866, a 21 anni. Davvero un bel giovane, non meraviglia che sia piaciuto tanto al suo popolo.

ルードヴィッヒ二世、1866年、21才。本当に美しい青年であり、人々に好かれていたのもうなずける。

The façade of Linderhof Palace, built in the neo-Rococo style in honour of the Bourbon Kings.

La façade du château Linderhof construit dans un style rococo imité en l'honneur des rois de la maison des Bourbons.

La facciata del Castello di Linderhof costruito in onore dei re borbonici a imitazione dello stile rococò.

リンダーホフ城の正面はブルボン王朝に敬意を表し、ロココスタイルを模倣して造ってある。

And still today, long after they have forgotten their other, more useful rulers, the Bavarian people hold moving commemorative celebrations and festivals in honour of King Ludwig; they set up societies to keep his memory alive and to maintain special memorial monuments. All of the members of these societies are firmly convinced that the King was in no way mad, or even mentally disturbed, nor was he gay; and they are all absolutely sure that he did not drown Dr Gudden, but was instead drowned by him. In the words of the popular King Ludwig Song, written shortly after his death:

"Und geheime Meuchelmörder,
deren Namen man nicht kennt,
habens ihn in'n See neingstessen,
indem sie ihn von hint angrennt."

"And secret murderers,
with names unknown,
did push him from behind
and in the lake he did drown."

There are some sixty or so King Ludwig fan clubs in existence, and by no means all of them were founded in the 19th century – most, in fact, were not set up until after the Second World War. The more picturesque representatives of these clubs have their hair and beards styled à la Ludwig, and the most faithful light candles on the King's sarcophagus; the industrious ones write bitter letters of complaint to the administration authorities about children or dogs swimming near Ludwig's Cross in the lake at Berg (where the King died). Apart from the fact that such activity is highly disrespectful, the King was known to have had an intense dislike of both children and dogs.

He also hated the Prussians; it is reported that whenever he passed a bust of the Emperor in Hohenschwangau Castle, he would spit at it. Swans, peacocks and horses, on the other hand, were most welcome. His greatest wish for the city of Munich was that it should be "set alight at all corners", and, when exhorted by his ministers to exercise restraint in his expenditure, he expressed a desire to exchange the Kingdom of Bavaria for another, more compliant country. "I spurn", he said, "the cheers and shouts of the crowds"; he set no store by meeting

The King in 1871. By now his front teeth had already fallen out, and so he never obliged photographers with a "cheese".

Le roi en 1871. Il a déjà perdu les dents de devant. Aussi évitait-il de trop sourire en présence d'un photographe.

Il re nel 1871. Gli mancavano già gli incisivi. Se fosse stato presente un fotografo, avrebbe evitato di sorridere pronunciando «cheese».

1871年の国王。この時すでに前歯が何本か欠けていた。その為、写真師がそばに居合わせた時には歯を見せて微笑むことは避けていた。

The last photograph of the King, taken in 1886. He weighed 120 kilos (at over 6 feet tall), and his waist measurement was 1.20 m.

La dernière photographie du roi en 1886. Il pèse à présent 120 kilos (pour 1 mètre 91 de grandeur); son tour de taille est de 1 mètre 20.

La prima fotografia del re nel 1886. Pesa 120 kg (per 1 metro e 91 di altezza), la sua pancia ha una circonferenza di 1,20 m.

国王の最後の写真、1886年。体重は120kg（身長 1メータ91センチ）で、胴囲は1メータ20センチである。

"Your image will live for ever in the faithful Bavarian heart", was the people's promise to their King.

« Ton image demeurera éternellement vivante dans le cœur fidèle des Bavarois » promit le peuple à son roi.

«La tua immagine vivrà in eterno nel fedele cuore bavarese» promise il popolo al suo re.

「陛下の肖像は忠誠なバイエルン魂の中に永遠に生き続けることでありましょう。」と人々は王に誓った。

his people, but instead preferred to ride out at night in a golden Rococo sleigh through the Bavarian woods, revelling in dreams of regal splendour and the power of kings. He loved to pore over plans for ever more magnificent castles – yet not, as the poet who wrote the Ludwig song naively suggested, "to the good of the people", but for his own exclusive enjoyment, in places where no-one but he would see them. For he feared that if ordinary people even set eyes on his castles, they would "soil and desecrate them".

How, then, did he win such love from his people? He was certainly the very antithesis of those tireless, hard-working rulers who devoted their lives to the good of their people and country. He was foolish, strange, expensive and squanderous, he was grotesque, bizarre, moody, unpredictable, and did not attempt in any way to find favour with his Bavaria. Pursued by malicious schemers, humiliated, and in the end murdered, he was to become a mysterious, tragic, spectacularly unhappy fairytale King – and one of the most important tourist attractions of the Free State of Bavaria.

The Early Years

LUDWIG FRIEDRICH WILHELM

Ludwig was born on August 25th, 1845, at half past midnight, in the Wittelsbacher's summer residence of Nymphenburg Palace, which at the time was outside the city of Munich. The omens for the birth of this strong healthy baby were good, for on the same day and at the same hour in 1786, one hundred years before Ludwig's death, his grandfather, Ludwig I, had been born. (False rumours immediately started that the future King had in fact been born two days earlier, and that the actual date of the birth had been falsified so as to coincide with that of the old King.)

On August 25th the Catholic church celebrates the Feast of Saint Ludwig. The young prince was thus one of those most unfortunate children whose name day and birthday fall on the same date, with the unhappy result that they can only have one celebration per year.

In addition to the name Ludwig, the boy was also christened Friedrich Wilhelm, as was customary for male offspring in the Prussian family of his mother. These latter names were, however, little used.

At the time of Ludwig's birth his father, Maximilian, was still Crown Prince. (He did not become King until 1848, the year in which Ludwig's brother Otto was born.) In a first flush of pride, Crown Prince Maximilian expressed "what a wonderful feeling it is to be a father", but this enthusiasm soon waned. His relationship with his sons was cool and distant; he had little understanding for them and it was said that he never laughed with them, instead only punishing them for misdemeanours and disobedience. He used to carry out the punishments himself, it hardly being suitable for common servants to clip the future King around the ear. Beatings were part and parcel of growing up, they were seen as an important means of education.

"The King", we learn from a Cabinet Secretary called Pfistermeister, "only saw his two sons, Prince Ludwig and Prince Otto, one or two times a day: at midday for the second breakfast and in the evening at the dinner table. He seldom saw them in the apartments in which they grew up. On the occasions he did see them he merely offered his hand in greeting and then made a hasty retreat." Later, as a thirty-year-old, Ludwig was to write that his father had always treated him "de haut en bas", at best acknowledging his presence "with one or two condescending, cold words in passing".

Ludwig's mother, Marie, was a Prussian princess, daughter of Prince Friedrich Wilhelm Carl. As a young woman she was quite pretty with blue eyes and dark hair, but with advancing years she became ever more corpulent.

She had a kind friendly nature, but was rather stupid, drab, simple, prosaic and quite without any musical or even intellectual interests. Content to spend her time tending to the flowers or engaged in needlework, she did not like the theatre and would declare with a certain pride that she never read a book. She loved the countryside in Upper Bavaria and went down in the tourist history of the region as the first woman Alpine walker from Berlin; she was often seen scrambling tirelessly up mountains with her royal offspring.

Strangely, although naive, kind mother types generally manage to establish good relationships even with exalted sons, mother Marie's contacts with her sons were far from satisfactory. Franz von Pfistermeister observed: "The Queen, too,

The two princes: Ludwig, aged five, and Otto, aged two, with their mother, Marie, and father, Maximilian, in the grounds of Hohenschwangau Castle.

Les princes, Louis, cinq ans, et Otto, deux ans, avec leur mère Marie et leur père Maximilien dans le parc du château de Hohenschwangau.

I principini, Ludwig di 5 anni, Otto di 2 con la madre Maria e il padre Massimiliano nel parco del Castello di Hohenschwangau.

王子たち。ルートヴィヒ5才、オットー2才。母マリー、父マクシミリアンとともにホーエンシュヴァンガウ城の庭園にて。

Next double page:
Ludwig II was born on August 25th, 1845, in the royal summer residence, the Palace of Nymphenburg.

Page double suivante:
Louis II est né le 25 août 1845 dans la résidence royale d'été, le château Nymphenburg.

Doppia pagina successiva:
Ludwig II nacque il 25 agosto 1845 nella residenza reale estiva del castello di Nymphenburg.

次ページ見開き：
王家の夏の離宮ニンフェンブルク城でルートヴィヒ　世は1845年8月25日に誕生した。

The five-year-old Crown Prince Ludwig at play, showing an early interest in architecture.

Le prince héritier Louis âgé de cinq ans en tant que tambour et architecte en herbe.

Il principe ereditario Ludwig a 5 anni in veste di tamburino e di piccolo costruttore.

5才の王子ルートヴィヒ。太鼓を叩く音楽家で、小さな建築家でもあった。

had little notion of how to form a good relationship with the Princes. She did visit them in their rooms more often (than the father), but was unable to behave with them in a way which children understand. And so no real fondness grew between them." Ludwig had little in common with his mother all his life. "My mother does not understand me in the least", he complained to Richard Wagner, and in 1876 he wrote: "As is befitting, I love and honour my mother, the Queen. Yet the impossibility of a close relationship with a nature such as hers is no fault of mine." In later years he grew to detest her, liking to refer to her as the "widow of my predecessor". As such, he believed, it was her place to honour him: "I am the monarch, and she is just the mother, and at the same time an underling."

The Princes' education lay in the hands of men of limited inspiration. From them they learned little apart from an appreciation of their status. The guiding principles in their education were a carefully maintained unworldliness and an unerring strictness. The boys were forced to rise early and suffer long hours of lessons each day; there were no sweets and pocket money was only granted in very modest amounts. Contacts with other children were not considered important. Gottfried von Böhm, the author of the generally recognised standard biography of King Ludwig, wrote: "The life the two Princes led was a very simple one. It was one of the commonly held misconceptions in the upper classes at that time, that children should never be allowed to eat their fill; as a result the future King was very happy when his faithful nurse, Lili, or some of the other servants brought him some food from the town, or gave him some of their own, more plentiful fare." All this was supposed to make the princes into industrious, duty-conscious rulers, and encourage them towards moderation and simplicity.

As we now know, this method failed miserably.

Character flaws which show themselves later in life can often be traced back to a joyless, loveless childhood, and it is interesting to wonder now in the case of King Ludwig, whether the reason why he spent money like water lay in the fact that as a child he was never given any? Or were the beatings he administered to his servants a memory of the countless punishments meted out to him by his own, unloved father? Perhaps his gluttony stemmed from childhood deprivation? Can his enthusiasm for all things concerned with the Bourbon Kings, the Order of the Knights of Saint George, the Orient and other types of masquerade be traced back

The two royal princes, in rather oversized suits, setting off on a mountain hike.

Les deux garçonnets royaux dans des costumes un peu amples lors du départ pour une randonnée en montagne.

I due rampolli reali, in abbigliamento un po' abbondante, mentre si avviano a una camminata in montagna.

2人の王子たち。山歩きでほころんだ少しだぶついた背広を着て。

From the royal family album: the princes in 1855.

Extrait de l'album de la famille royale de Bavière: les princes vers 1855.

Dall'album di famiglia dei reali bavaresi: i principi nel 1855.

バイエルン王室のアルバムから：王子たち、1855年頃。

to his boyhood days of having to wear sobre, often ill-fitting clothes? And could his habit of turning night into day have been a reaction against all those childhood years of having to get up early? Evidently this is a rich seam for amateur psychological speculation.

Other reports of the time when Ludwig was still Crown Prince tell that the young princes, Ludwig and Otto, were "the most handsome and attractive children one could wish for". Ludwig was an intelligent pupil, but did not apply his talents equally in all subjects. Already at a young age he was known to be quite adept with the building blocks. He had not the least gift for music. "For his former piano teacher the day on which he gave the last lesson to the Crown Prince was a most fortunate one, because of the lack of talent of his illustrious pupil." (Richard Wagner was also later to confirm that "The King is quite without musical talent, possessing only a poetical spirit.") On the other hand young Ludwig was an excellent swimmer and horseman. Once, we are told, he even tried to execute his brother Otto for insubordination, but fortunately was discovered in time and stopped. During the summer months Ludwig enjoyed staying at Hohenschwangau Castle.

The princes, Ludwig and Otto, with their mother, seated at a somewhat sparsely laid table.

Les princes Louis et Otto avec leur mère Marie lors d'un modeste repas.

I principi Ludwig e Otto con la madre Maria al parco pranzo.

ルートヴィヒ王子とオットー王子、母マリーと慎ましやかな食事。

Königin Marie von Bayern
und deren Kinder, die späteren
Könige Ludwig II. und Otto I.

A fresco in Hohenschwangau Castle showing the departure of Lohengrin.

La fresque du château de Hohenschwangau montre les adieux de Lohengrin.

L'affresco del castello di Hohenschwangau mostra il congedo di Lohengrin.

ホーエンシュヴァンガウ城のフレスコ画はローエングリーン（白鳥の騎士）の別れを表している。

Hohenschwangau

TRULY A FAIRYTALE CASTLE

In 1832 Crown Prince Maximilian had acquired possession of a 700-year-old ruin called Schwanstein Castle. Enchanted by its superb location with a view over the waters of Alpsee towards the mountains of Allgäu, he decided he would "restore its original mediaeval form" and use it as a summer residence.

This, of course, was to be no historically faithful reconstruction – people were not so narrow-minded in those days. Instead he commissioned a theatre set designer(!), Dominik Quaglio, to create a dreamy, fairytale knight's castle, in keeping with nineteenth century romantic notions of what such castles were like. It was to be wonderfully neo-Gothic, and as fantastic and picturesque as possible, with decorative towers and turrets, oriels, portals, balconies, pillars, crenellated parapets – an image altogether so enchanting that when the King's father, Ludwig I, saw it for the first time in 1844, he cried out in amazement: "Hohenschwangau is truly a fairytale castle!"

The rooms were decorated with colourful wall paintings, mostly designs by Moritz von Schwind, depicting noble scenes from old heroic sagas and tales from the Crusades. Here we see "Dietrich's flight from Verona", and Erka, Queen of the Huns, arming her sons; here, too, Authari strikes his axe into an oak tree and Armida carries Rinaldo off in her carriage drawn by dragons. Here in this castle, Ludwig found fuel for his mediaeval fantasies; here father and son could have come closer together in their shared love of mythology and legend. But perhaps the encounters were more along the lines of: "Papa, is that Lohengrin the Knight?" – "It is indeed, and here stands Elsa, weeping. And now he must go away with his beloved swan, because Elsa was too inquisitive. Therefore, you should never ask too many questions..." This would hardly have formed the basis for a fruitful father-son relationship.

Hohenschwangau was not built by King Ludwig, but by his father.

Hohenschwangau n'a pas été construit par le roi Louis, mais par son père.

Hohenschwangau non è stata costruita da Ludwig, bensì dal padre.

ホーエンシュヴァンガウ城はルートヴィヒ　世ではなく、彼の父によって建設された。

The royal insignia of Bavaria – crown, orb and sceptre. They symbolise the dignity of the crown.

Les insignes royaux de la Bavière avec la couronne, le globe impérial et le sceptre. Ils symbolisent la dignité royale.

Le insegne reali bavaresi con la corona, il globo imperiale e lo scettro. Simboleggiano la maestà reale.

王冠、十字架つきの宝珠、王しゃくから成るバイエルンの表章。これらは王の威厳の象徴である。

Royal Duties

I, The King

At the age of 18½, and still not yet completed his schooling, Ludwig, attired in the colonel's uniform of his infantry regiment, ascended to the Bavarian throne following the sudden death of his father.

In the early days he fulfilled his royal duties with admirable dedication. He conferred with ministers and secretaries of state, he held audiences, and allowed himself to be cheered by his people; he governed conscientiously, albeit with little ability. The Austrian envoy, Count Blome, wrote: "Of political matters, in particular current issues, he knows even less than can be expected for his age." This situation could nevertheless have improved over time, but unfortunately the same happened to the King as to many sons who step into their father's shoes: he did not like the work. Richard Wagner noted: "An inconceivably senseless education has managed to awaken in the youth a deep, and as yet completely insurmountable, aversion to any serious involvement with the affairs of state; instead, in deep contempt, almost disgust, for all concerned, he simply allows these matters to take their own course, following established routines performed by officials of long standing." The King withdrew to the mountains, taking refuge in Hohenschwangau, and by October of the year of his accession the Minister for External Affairs was to be found standing at the gates of the castle, "begging that the King should take up his duties, and not simply follow his inclinations". The theologian Ignaz von Döllinger remarked: "Our royal master lives and breathes in the world of heroic saga, of poetry, music

"Ich, der König" (I, the King), an excerpt from the King's diary. He was fascinated by his own rank.

« Moi, le Roi » inscrivit dans son journal le roi fasciné par sa propre majesté.

«Io, il Re» annotò nel suo diario il re, affascinato dalla sua dignità.

「世は王なり。」王は自分の威厳に酔いしれて日記にしたためた。

The most famous portrait of the young King, in general's uniform and coronation robe. Painted by Ferdinand Piloty in 1865.

Le plus célèbre portrait du jeune roi. Ferdinand Piloty le peignit en 1865 en uniforme de général et manteau de sacre.

L'immagine più famosa del giovane re. Ferdinand Piloty lo dipinse nel 1865 in uniforme da generale e col manto dell'incoronazione.

若き王の最も有名な絵。
1865年フェルディナント・ピロティ作。
将軍の制服に即位式のコートを着ている。

Next double page: The highest point on the King Ludwig Path: the "Wieskirche", the most important of the Swabian-Bavarian Rococo churches.

Page double suivante: Le point culminant de la vie du roi Louis: l'Eglise Wies, la plus importante des églises rococo souabes-bavaroises.

**Doppia pagina successiva:
Il culmine della via di re Ludwig: il Santuario di Wies, la più significative delle chiese rococò svevo-bavaresi.**

次ページ見開き：
ルートヴィヒ王通りの高台：ヴィース教会、シュヴァーベン－バイエルンのロココ教会のなかで最も立派な教会である。

So lang dem Heer das
deutsche Banner weht,
Sei Der geehrt der es zuerst erhöht,
So lang der Bau des Reichs die
Zinne trägt,
Sei Dem gedankt, der treu den Grund gelegt,
Der mit der Krone Zier geschmückt das Dach
Und sprach: dem Kaiser huldigt Wittelsbach.
Heil dem
Ludwig
dem
Deutschen
Bayerns
heil

The victory march of the Bavarian troops in Munich on July 16th, 1871, after the Franco-German War.

L'entrée triomphale des troupes bavaroises à Munich le 16 juillet 1871 après la guerre franco-allemande.

L'ingresso trionfale delle truppe bavaresi a Monaco il 16 luglio 1871 dopo la guerra franco-tedesca.

1871年7月16日、独仏戦争後のバイエルン軍のミュンヘンへの凱旋。

and drama. … The outside world and prosaic everyday concerns do not interest him in the least, he seeks to distance himself as much as possible from them."

In 1866 when the war against Prussia was imminent, he was to be found with his adjutant and a groom on Roseninsel, an island in the middle of Lake Starnberg; he wished to speak to no-one, preferring instead to spend his time setting off fireworks.

He complained about the "appallingly dreadful duties which at times simply cannot be endured", and was occasionally heard to mention abdication. His political abilities were not such that he could point with pride to any great successes: in 1866 he took the side of Austria in the Seven Weeks' War, in which Prussia soundly defeated Austria. After this he was forced to enter into a defensive alliance with the victorious enemy. After the Franco-German War, against his will and following an unsuccessful attempt to avoid the matter entirely by feigning illness, he wrote the so-called "Imperial letter" to the Prussian King, Wilhelm I. In this letter he exhorted Wilhelm to take on the title of "Deutscher Kaiser", German Emperor, a move which was to mean the loss of most of the sovereign rights of his own country, Bavaria. It would not, in fact, have altered the course of German history if the letter had not been written. Nevertheless Ludwig was extremely upset. "What misfortune", he complained "that I should be King in this time and be myself compelled in the interests of Bavaria, to make this painful sacrifice."

From that point onwards he withdrew even more from his governmental duties, with the attitude: "A King is never obliged to do anything!" He turned his back more and more on the "unholy outside world" and sank into a fantasy dream world which was more in tune with his vision of an ideal kingdom. He became obsessed with notions of the absolutist Bourbon monarchs, Louis XIV and Louis XV; to Ludwig these Kings were not only

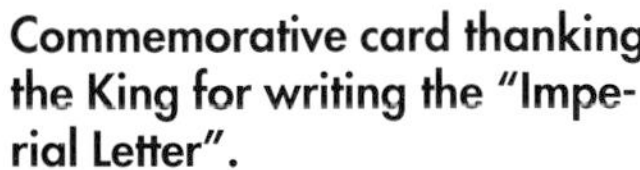

Commemorative card thanking the King for writing the "Imperial Letter".

Feuille commémorative pour le roi Louis en remerciement d'avoir écrit la lettre impériale.

Foglio commemorativo per Re Ludwig per ringraziamento di avere scritto la lettera imperiale.

ルートヴィヒ王の記念画。皇帝書簡を執筆した事に感謝の意を表して。

the perfect embodiment of royal power and opulence, but they became his role models. On night-time excursions he took to wearing majestic robes in royal blue velvet, after the fashion of Louis XIV, with a velvet beret and white ostrich feather; he possessed hundreds of books about life at the Bourbon court and in his royal theatre he could immerse himself in the atmosphere of Versailles in plays specially commissioned on this theme. These performances were put on exclusively for the King, accompanied by one or two selected guests; this was the only way he could be safe from the prying eyes of an inquisitive public. Betwen 1872 and 1875 209 seperate performances were held for the King. The reason why Ludwig wanted these private showings was quite a valid one: "I cannot possibly fully enjoy a theatre performance", he said "as long as people continue to stare at me during the whole show, even training their opera glasses on me to get a closer look. I am there to observe, not to be observed." (The idea of darkening the auditorium was not introduced until a later date).

Ludwig's Linderhof and Herrenchiemsee Palaces were homages to the Bourbon rulers. On days when he dined alone, he used to invite them along, and had his servants prepare and serve supper for three or four persons; on these occasions he would drink and dine in high spirits in the company of Madame Pompadour and the Marquise de Maintenon and their Kings. In these hours his dreams of divine right and absolute majesty were fulfilled.

The Prussian King Wilhelm I on a visit to Hohenschwangau. He is seated in the carriage between Ludwig and Marie.

Le roi prussien Guillaume Ier lors d'une visite à Hohenschwangau. On le reconnaît dans la calèche entre Louis et Marie.

Il Re prussiano Guglielmo I in visita a Hohenschwangau. E' riconoscibile nella carrozza tra Ludwig e Maria.

プロシア王ヴィルヘルム　世、ホーエンシュヴァンガウ城を訪問した際。馬車の上、ルートヴィヒとマリーの間に見える。

Next double page:
The King also had his eye on Wörth Island in Staffelsee as a possible site for his Bavarian Versailles.

Page double suivante:
Le roi avait également projeté de construire son Versailles bavarois sur l'Ile de Wörth du Staffelsee.

Doppia pagina successiva:
Il Re aveva già pensato anche all'isola di Wörth nel lago di Staffel come terreno da costruzione della sua Versailles bavarese.

次ページ見開き：
シュタフェル湖に浮かぶヴェアト島でも王は彼のバイエルンのヴェルサイユのために敷地をすでに用意していた。

Betrothed

No Woman Can Resist You

"You are a fortunate man," the old King Ludwig I is reported to have said to his grandson, "no woman can resist you." And indeed, the ladies were much taken with this beautiful young king, but their success was only moderate: in contrast to his grandfather, who had quite a reputation as a ladies' man, Ludwig was little drawn to them. He could be galant and gracious, and, when the occasion arose, would present them with flowers and other gifts, but that was about the extent of his involvement.

He flirted with a few actresses, and had a close, lifelong friendship with Empress Elisabeth of Austria, but all of these relationships were purely platonic. "Only emotional love is permitted, but physical love is cursed", he noted in his diary.

However, it was practically a King's duty to marry a beautiful princess and have children; this was expected by his people and was required for reasons of state.

Opposite Berg Castle, towards the southwest on the other side of the Lake Starnberg was another castle, at Possenhofen. This was the home of Ludwig's uncle, Duke Maximilian and his wife, Ludovika. Their daughter, Sissi, often came to visit her parents and her younger sister, Duchess Sophie-Charlotte, who also lived here. Nowadays Possenhofen Castle has been converted into exclusive private apartments.

Sophie was a pretty girl, two years younger than Ludwig; she was blonde, slim, blue-eyed and loved Wagner's music. Their friendship grew, and Ludwig often visited her. Finally, in 1867 after a court ball, he resolved rather hastily to marry her.

Ludwig brought his bride-to-be many expensive presents, once even bringing the Queen's crown for her to try on; he also had rooms in the Residence Palace specially decorated for her. However, his interest would often wane and he would disappear on his own, either to Wartburg Castle, to Paris or simply to the theatre. His letters to her were friendly, but

Contemporary postcard showing the King and Empress Elisabeth (Sissi) in the rose garden on Roseninsel in Lake Starnberg.

Carte postale d'antan: le roi et l'impératrice Elisabeth (Sissi) dans la corbeille aux roses de l'Ile des Roses du Lac de Starnberg.

Cartolina d'epoca: il Re e la Regina Elisabeth (Sissi) nell'aiuola circolare di rose della Roseninsel nel lago Starnberg.

当時の葉書：国王と女帝エリザベート（シシー）
シュタルンベルク湖に浮かぶローゼン島の円形薔薇花壇にて。

dispassionate in tone: "Of all the women who live, you are the dearest to me. Among my relatives I like Wilhelm the best, and Künsberg is one of my most favourite servants…" She could embroider, and would sing Wagner arias to him in a pale, sweet voice; sometimes he kissed her, but only on the forehead. He knew very well that this behaviour was not quite what was expected, but he had very chaste principles, as was revealed once in a remark to one of his ministers, Mr von den Pfordten: "In the case of most young people, sensuality is mixed up in their relationships with the opposite sex; I condemn this." As the wedding drew nearer

King Maximilian II had this small, Pompeiian-style castle built on Roseninsel.

Ce petit château de style pompéien fut construit par le roi Max II sur l'Ile des Roses.

Re Max II fece costruire questo piccolo castello in stile pompeiano sulla Roseninsel.

このポンペイスタイルの小城はマックス世王がローゼン島に造らせたもの。

On his paddle-steamer "Tristan" Ludwig liked to travel from Berg to the romantic Roseninsel. He also gave receptions here.

Louis aimait à se rendre de Berg à la romantique Ile des Roses sur son bateau à aubes « Tristan ». Il y donnait également des réceptions.

Col suo piroscafo a ruote «Tristan» Ludwig si recava volentieri da Berg alla romantica Roseninsel. Qui teneva anche ricevimenti.

外輪船「トリスタン」でベルクからロマンチックなローゼン島まで渡ることをルートヴィヒは好んだ。またここローゼン島でレセプションを催した。

Empress Elisabeth of Austria was the sister of Ludwig's bride-to-be, Sophie. She was outraged when Ludwig broke off the engagement.

L'impératrice Elisabeth d'Autriche était la soeur de la fiancée de Louis et fut très indignée lorsque Louis rompit ses fiançailles.

La regina Elisabeth d'Austria era la sorella della fidanzata di Ludwig, Sophie, e fu mossa da enorme sdegno quando Ludwig ruppe il fidanzamento.

オーストリアのエリザベート女帝はルートヴィヒの婚約者ゾフィーの姉でルートヴィヒが婚約を破棄した時には激怒した。

Ludwig became more and more ill at ease. He postponed the date several times, from August 25th (his birthday) to October 12th, the date on which his parents and grandparents had married; then he decided that perhaps November 12th would be more suitable, later still changing his mind in favour of the November 28th. Finally he expressed a preference for a December wedding. But no doubt this, too, would also have been subject to a further postponement.

"But on October 10th the King finally broke off the engagement", reports the

F. Wanderer inv.
A. Meermann sc. & impr.
Zur Vermählung Jhrer Majestäten
KÖNIGS LUDWIG II. UND KÖNIGIN SOPHIE VON BAYERN.

A commemorative card to mark the royal marriage that never took place.

Feuille commémorative en souvenir du mariage du roi qui n'eut jamais lieu.

Foglio commemorativo a ricordo di nozze reali che non ebbero mai luogo.

実際に催されることはついになかった国王の結婚式の記念画。

tour guide of Herrenchiemsee Palace. "Because his future parents-in-law had put more and more pressure on him to marry. And so in the end he didn't want to any more."

The fact was that the King had for a long time not been so keen on the idea, and was quite glad to be presented an ultimatum by the father-in-law: the choice was between marrying Sophie on November 28th or calling off the engagement altogether. With a sense of great relief and pleasure, he threw Sophie's bust out of the window and wrote to his bride: "Your dreadful father is tearing us apart."

Shortly after he sent her a short, supplementary note to this, stating that his feelings for her were more a kind of "faithful, heartfelt brotherly love", and "not the kind of love which is needed for the union of marriage".

However, he did galantly seek to offer his bride some consolation, indicating that the situation was not altogether hopeless: "If within one year you should have found no-one with whom you think you could be happier than with me, a situation which, I think, is not impossible, then we could come together once again for ever more, provided that you still want to." Sophie did not take up this

Sophie and her chaste royal cousin, Ludwig, made a handsome couple.

Sophie et son chaste cousin royal Louis auraient formé un beau couple.

Sophie e il suo casto cugino regale Ludwig sarebbero stati davvero una bella coppia.

ゾフィーと純潔の王家の従兄弟ルートヴィヒは美しいカップルとなるはずだった。

Commemorative coins marking the royal marriage of Ludwig and Sophie are nowadays a rarity.

Les médailles commémoratives de mariage avec les portraits de Louis et Sophie sont aujourd'hui des raretés.

Le monete commemorative delle nozze con i ritratti di Ludwig e Sophie sono oggi una rarità.

ルートヴィヒとゾフィーの肖像の付いた結婚記念硬貨は今日では稀少品である。

Previous double page: Neuschwanstein was built almost exactly in line with plans devised by Christian Jank, a theatre set designer.

Page double précédente: Le château de Neuschwanstein a été presque construit exactement d'après les plans du peintre de théâtre Christian Jank.

Doppia pagina precedente: Il castello di Neuschwanstein fu costruito quasi esattamente uguale a come ne aveva tratteggiato lo schizzo l'architetto scenografo Christian Jank.

前ページ見開き：
劇場画家クリスチアン・ヤンクが立案したのとほとんど同じ様にノイシュヴァンシュタン城は建築された。

The jilted royal bride, Sophie. She died in 1897 in a fire at a charity event in Paris.

Sophie, la future épouse dédaignée. Elle perdit la vie en 1897 à Paris lors d'un incendie qui se déclara lors d'une vente de charité.

La fidanzata del re rifiutata, Sophie. Nel 1897 perse la vita nell'incendio di una fiera di beneficenza a Parigi.

婚約を破棄されたゾフィー。1897年パリの慈善音楽会での火事で死亡。

kind-hearted offer, but married Duke Ferdinand von Alençon before the year was up.

The King, however, was greatly relieved: "Sophie written off", was the entry in his diary. "The dark cloud hanging over me has been swept away. I yearned for freedom, longed for the painful nightmare to come to an end." – To Richard Wagner, he wrote: "Now, all is well again! I feel resurrected, recovered from a life-threatening illness, ... the black ribbon of mourning which has been hanging over me in recent times is now torn down..." – The happy end of an unhappy engagement.

A painter's image of Ludwig, clad as the "Swan Knight", Lohengrin, being rowed through the Linderhof grotto.

C'est ainsi, d'après le peintre, que Louis se promenait en barque dans sa grotte de Linderhof, tel Lohengrin, le chevalier aux cygnes.

Così come l'aveva immaginato il pittore, come il cavaliere di cigni Lohengrin, Ludwig si fece immortalare remando attraverso la grotta di Linderhof.

この画家は、ルートヴィヒが白鳥の騎士ローエングリーンとしてリンダーホーフ城の鍾乳洞の湖を漕ぎ進む姿を表現している。

Richard Wagner

BELOVED ONE, HOLY ONE!

In April 1864, soon after his accession to the throne, Ludwig sent his Cabinet Secretary, Pfistermeister, into the wide world to search for Richard Wagner, who was at the time staying in a succession of temporary abodes somewhere between Zurich, Vienna and Stuttgart, fleeing from his creditors. Wagner's "Ring", his "Meistersinger" were still incomplete; "Tristan and Isolde" had not yet been performed on any stage.

Pfistermeister found Wagner and brought him back to his King on May 4th.

The King bestowed upon him friendship, grace, favour, deep admiration and love, and promised: "I shall banish for ever the lower concerns of your daily life"; he also took care of the higher concerns, by paying off Wagner's countless debts, presenting him with a house on Briennerstrasse in Munich, financing the immoderate luxury with which the artist surrounded himself, and writing enthusiastic letters: "Beloved one, Holy one! I am like a spark longing to be enflamed and illuminated in the rays of your sun…" (nothing like this occurred to him when writing to his bride, Sophie). His praise of Wagner was almost a litany: "My dear friend, the only source of joy from my tender young days, you spoke to my heart like no other, you are my best teacher and educator."

The King even wanted to have a theatre built especially for Wagner. It was to be situated in Munich, on the right bank of the Isar, below the Maximilianeum. The design was drawn up by the famous architect, Gottfried Semper, and the proposal also included a new road which would lead directly to the theatre from the Residence Palace over a new bridge. The costs for the project were estimated at six million guilders.

However, the Cabinet and all those who considered thrift to be a virtue opposed the plan and succeeded in sabotaging it, with the result that the King had to give up his idea. He was so offended by this that from then on he hated that "unholy town" with a vengeance, escaping from it as often as he could and gracing the mountains instead with his castles.

Wagner's music was very popular in Munich and the premiere of Tristan and Isolde in June 1865 was a huge success.

The thing that the people, courtiers and politicians, nobility, clergy and the rest of the royal family did not like, however, was Wagner himself, and his squanderous ways which he unabashedly allowed the King to finance; they disliked the increasing influence he had over Ludwig, which extended far beyond the realms of music theatre, and his attempts to bring this influence to bear in political matters.

On December 1st, 1865 Minister von der Pfordten thus saw fit to warn the King: "This man who dares to maintain that the faithful and true men of the Royal Cabinet do not enjoy the least respect from the Bavarian people, is instead himself held in much greater contempt by all sides of the populace – that very populace from whom the throne seeks support and in whom alone that support can be found. This same man is despised because of his ingratitude and treachery towards benefactors and friends, because of his dissolute high living and wasteful indulgence, and because of the unashamed way in which he takes advantage of Your Majesty's favour. Your most faithful servant, the undersigned, wishes in no way to diminish or demean Your Majesty's enthusiasm for art and poetry, but he cannot disassociate himself from the general con-

Caricature of the wasteful Wagner. It is said that in 17 months he obtained about 100,000 guilders from the royal coffers.

Caricature du dépensier Wagner. Il est supposé avoir obtenu presque 100.000 gulden de la caisse de la cour en l'espace de 17 mois.

Caricatura del dissipatore Wagner. In 17 mesi deve avere ritirato quasi 100 000 fiorini dalle casse di corte.

浪費家ワグナーの風刺画。17か月の間に10万グルデンほどもの金を王宮金庫から引出させたという。

A design by the famous architect, Gottfried Semper, for a proposed King Ludwig's Wagner Festival Theatre.

C'est ainsi que devait se présenter l'opéra Wagner du roi Louis d'après les plans du célèbre architecte Gottfried Semper.

Secondo i progetti del famoso architetto Gottfried Semper, così avrebbe dovuto essere il teatro dei festival wagneriani di Re Ludwig.

ルートヴィヒ王のワグナー歌劇場は高名な建築家ゴットフリード・ゼンパーの案に基づいて、このような外観になるはずであった。

The master plays his "heavenly music" and the King listens with rapturous attention.

Le maître joue, le roi tend l'oreille, charmé par cette « musique céleste ».

Il maestro suona, il re ascolta rapito la sua «musica celestiale».

巨匠がピアノを弾き、王は彼の「天の音楽」に恍惚として耳を傾ける。

The premieres of Wagner's operas, the "Meistersinger", "Rheingold" and the "Valkyries" were held in the Nationaltheater in Munich.

Les opéras wagnériens « Tristan », les « Maîtres chanteurs de Nuremberg », « L'Or du Rhin » et la « Walkyrie » furent représentés pour la première fois au Théâtre National de Munich.

Nel Teatro Nazionale di Monaco si tennero le prime delle opere di Wagner «Tristano», i «Mastri Cantori», «L'oro del Reno» e la «Walkiria».

ミュンヘンの国立劇場ではワグナーのオペラ「トリスタン」、「マイスタージンガー」、「ラインの黄金」、そして「ヴァルキューレ」が初演された。

viction that this enthusiasm is being misused and exploited by an unworthy person."

This did indeed give the King pause for thought, and, faced with the choice between people and composer, he chose the former, under pressure from a Cabinet of ministers who, to a man, were threatening to resign: "I want to show my dear people, that their trust, their love is more important to me than anything."

Angered, Wagner left Munich for Switzerland on December 10th, 1865. His continued comfortable circumstances in his new home near Lucerne were, however, assured by a generous grant of 8000 guilders per year from the King.

The friendship between King and composer continued to flourish at a distance. They wrote letters to one another, the King visiting Wagner in Switzerland and Wagner visiting the King on Roseninsel and coming to Munich for the city's premiere of the Meistersinger. At times the relationship cooled, at others it rekindled, and in 1873 when Wagner needed money to complete his Festival Theatre in Bayreuth the King was again very generous in his support, despite very heavy financial commitments in his castle building projects (which were already costing much more than was available in the royal coffers).

On February 13th, 1883 Richard Wagner died in Venice, at the age of 69. Ludwig had once written to him: "And when we are both long since gone from this earth, our work will still stand as a beacon throughout posterity." "Our work"? – The King was perhaps not so far from the truth. What would have become of Wagner if Ludwig had not supported him? "The artist for whom the world now mourns", he said proudly, "was first recognised by me – I was the one to rescue him for the world."

This caricature expresses the close relationship between the King and the composer.

Cette caricature souhaite exprimer les liens étroits entre le roi et le compositeur.

Questa caricatura vuole esprimere lo stretto rapporto tra il re e il compositore.

この風刺画は国王と作曲家の密接な間柄を表現している。

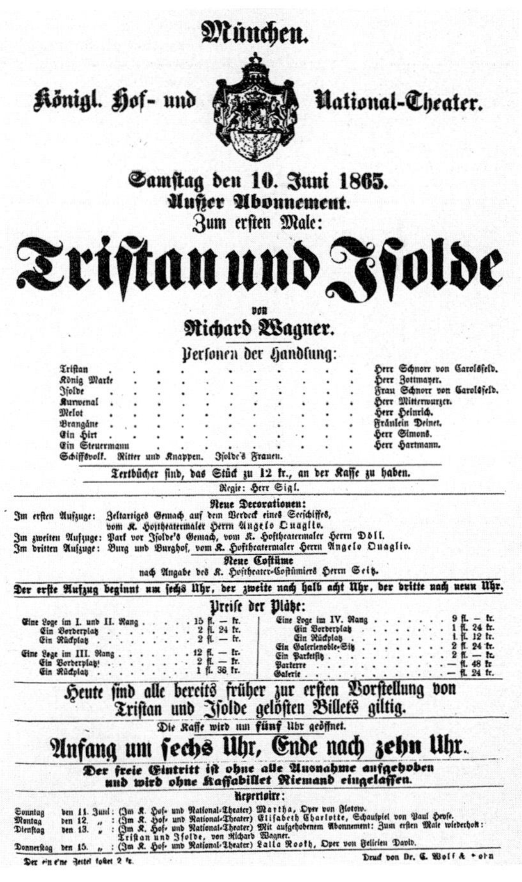

München.

Königl. Hof- und National-Theater.

Samstag den 10. Juni 1865.
Außer Abonnement.
Zum ersten Male:

Tristan und Isolde

von

Richard Wagner.

Personen der Handlung:

Tristan	Herr Schnorr von Carolsfeld.
König Marke	Herr Zottmayer.
Isolde	Frau Schnorr von Carolsfeld.
Kurwenal	Herr Mitterwurzer.
Melot	Herr Heinrich.
Brangäne	Fräulein Deinet.
Ein Hirt	Herr Simons.
Ein Steuermann	Herr Hartmann.

Schiffsvolk. Ritter und Knappen. Isolde's Frauen.

Textbücher sind, das Stück zu 12 kr., an der Kasse zu haben.

Regie: Herr Sigl.

Neue Decorationen:

Im ersten Aufzuge: Zeltartiges Gemach auf dem Verdeck eines Seeschiffes, vom K. Hoftheatermaler Herrn Angelo Quaglio.
Im zweiten Aufzuge: Park vor Isolde's Gemach, vom K. Hoftheatermaler Herrn Döll.
Im dritten Aufzuge: Burg und Burghof, vom K. Hoftheatermaler Herrn Angelo Quaglio.

Neue Costüme
nach Angabe des K. Hoftheater-Costümiers Herrn Seitz.

Der erste Aufzug beginnt um sechs Uhr, der zweite nach halb acht Uhr, der dritte nach neun Uhr.

Preise der Plätze:

Eine Loge im I. und II. Rang	15 fl. — kr.
Ein Vorderplatz	2 fl. 24 kr.
Ein Rückplatz	2 fl. — kr.
Eine Loge im III. Rang	12 fl. — kr.
Ein Vorderplatz	2 fl. — kr.
Ein Rückplatz	1 fl. 36 kr.
Eine Loge im IV. Rang	9 fl. — kr.
Ein Vorderplatz	1 fl. 24 kr.
Ein Rückplatz	1 fl. 12 kr.
Ein Galerienoble-Sitz	2 fl. 24 kr.
Ein Parketsitz	2 fl. — kr.
Parterre	— fl. 48 kr.
Galerie	— fl. 24 kr.

Heute sind alle bereits früher zur ersten Vorstellung von Tristan und Isolde gelösten Billets giltig.

Die Kasse wird um fünf Uhr geöffnet.

Anfang um sechs Uhr, Ende nach zehn Uhr.

Der freie Eintritt ist ohne alle Ausnahme aufgehoben und wird ohne Kassabillet Niemand eingelassen.

Repertoire:

Sonntag den 11. Juni: (Im K. Hof- und National-Theater) Martha, Oper von Flotow.
Montag den 12. „ : (Im K. Hof- und National-Theater) Elisabeth Charlotte, Schauspiel von Paul Heyse.
Dienstag den 13. „ : (Im K. Hof- und National-Theater) Mit aufgehobenem Abonnement: Zum ersten Male wiederholt: Tristan und Isolde, von Richard Wagner.
Donnerstag den 15. „ : (Im K. Hof- und National-Theater) Lalla Rookh, Oper von Felicien David.

Der einzelne Zettel kostet 2 kr.

Druck von Dr. C. Wolf & Sohn

Theatre bill for the triumphal Tristan premiere on June 10th, 1865 in the "Hof- und Nationaltheater" in Munich.

L'affiche de théâtre de la première de Tristan qui fut un triomphe le 10 juin 1865 au Théâtre de la Cour et National à Munich.

Il programma della trionfale prima del Tristano il 10 giugno 1865 nel teatro «Hof- und Nationaltheater» di Monaco.

1865年6月10日のトリスタン初演の演劇プログラム。ミュンヘン宮廷国立劇場

Previous double page:
The King loved to ride out at night on his sleigh. This majestic royal sleigh is now on display at the Marstallmuseum in Nymphenburg Palace.

Page double précédente:
Le roi aimait les excursions nocturnes. Son traîneau d'apparat se trouve aujourd'hui au Musée Marstall du Nymphenburg.

Doppia pagina precedente:
Il re amava le gite notturne. La sua lussuosa slitta è oggi conservata nel museo delle scuderie di Nymphenburg.

前ページ見開き：
国王は夜の遠出を愛した。王の豪華なそりは今日ニンフェンブルクのマールシュタール博物館に飾られている。

Retreat

THE DISAPPEARING MONARCH!

At times, it was said, the King was really nice – he would give his servants presents, pat young shepherd boys on the head and conduct pleasant conversations with famous artists. The general populace, as such, however, he considered a nuisance, particularly when present in great masses. "Can a people not show their love for their King other than always scraping and bowing in front of him?" he complained, "I cannot bear being stared at by thousands of people and having to ask them questions and feign interest in their answers."

One can symphathise with him. His reaction to this situation was, however, not in keeping with royal manners: he retreated to his hunting lodges and castles and "into the natural landscape and pure air of the mountains", where he lived in his own world of poetry and fantasy; seldom did he venture out for public engagements. The people of Munich had to accustom themselves to celebrating their openings of parliament and their Oktoberfests without their King. Toothache,

An artificial lake in an artificial grotto in the grounds of Linderhof Palace.

Lac artificiel dans la grotte de stalactites artificielle dans le parc de Linderhof.

Lago artificiale nella grotta artificiale con stalattiti nel parco di Linderhof.

リンダーホーフ城の庭にある人工鍾乳洞の中の人造湖。

"One morning, in true Bavarian style,
the city of Munich from its sleep did stir
Its head was sore, so it tarried awhile
Its eyes to open it did defer.

But a thunderous piece of news
Shot into its sleepy ear
Causing it with much ado
To leap out of its cosy lair."

"Bavarians! Awake!" it did declare,
"Your ruler has gone, he's taken flight.
A search of castles here and there
has not brought him yet to light."

What news! What tidings!
A worried look was seen to appear
As they hastened to consult their friends
At the inn, over a glass of beer. …

"Has he perhaps fled into the hills,
To join the shepherds there,
And refresh his many ills
In the cool, clear mountain air?

Or perhaps into the forest he has gone,
With nymphs and fairies to consort?
But, fear not, the sound of his horn
Will soon reveal his secret hide-out. …"

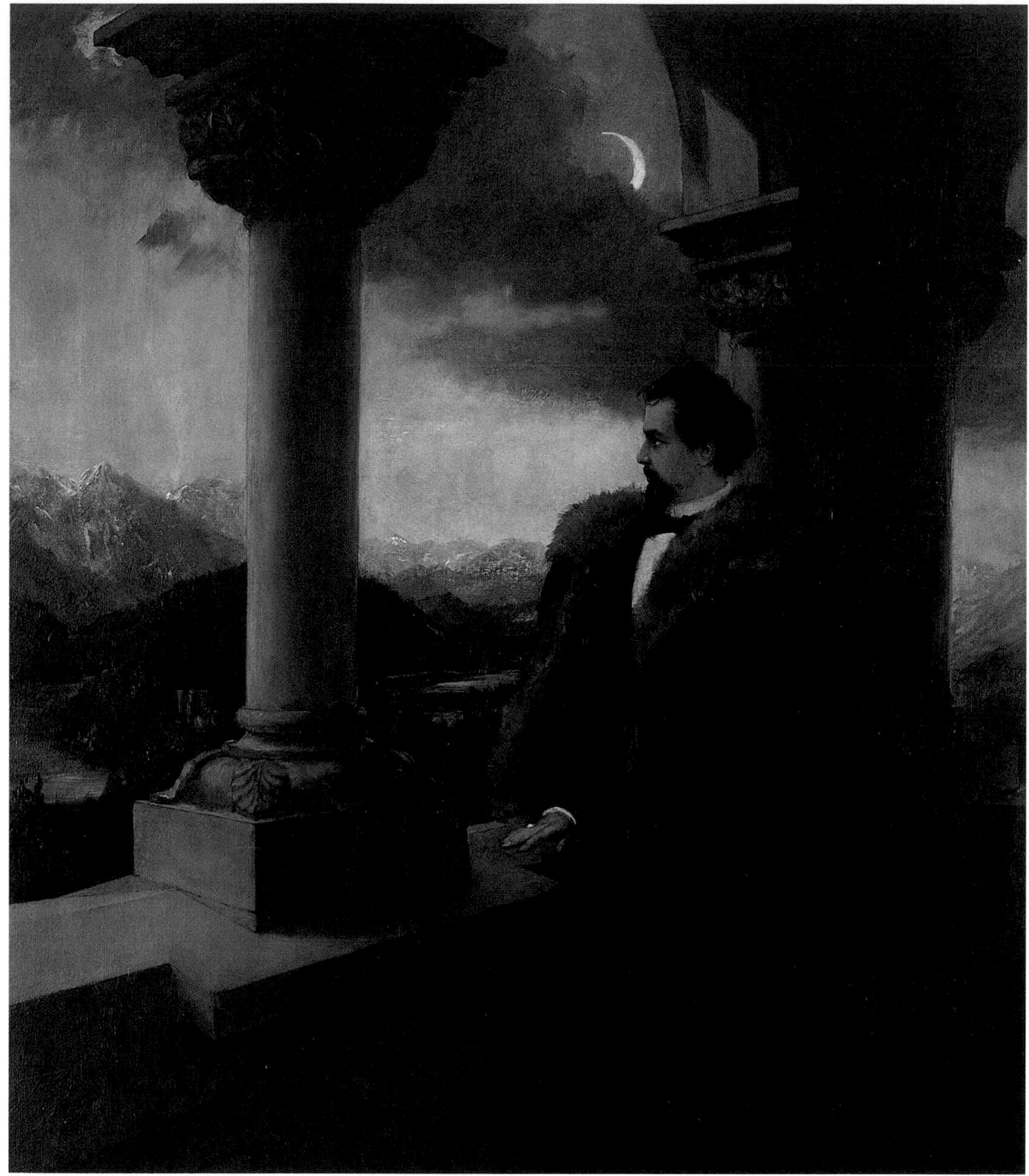

The King on the balcony of the Throne Room in Neuschwanstein at night. He loved the moon and the darkness.

Le roi sur le balcon de la salle du trône de Neuschwanstein la nuit. Il aimait la lune et les ténèbres.

Il Re sul balcone della sala del trono verso Neuschwanstein, di notte. Amava la luna e l'oscurità.

夜のノイシュヴァンシュタインの玉座の間のバルコニーの上の王。彼は月と闇を愛した。

facial swellings, catarrh and general malaise regularly prevented his attendance.

However, Ludwig put in a surprise appearance at the 1874 Corpus Christi procession. This "appearance of his Royal Majesty in the fullness of his manly strength and beauty", to quote a local newspaper, had "made the most favourable and joyful impression on the whole assembled populace". But he didn't stay long, and very soon after the celebrations he set off again, without informing anyone, and leaving behind a most disconcerted populace to celebrate the King's birthday without him. He had gone, as it later transpired, to Paris. Commenting on this strange affair, the Berlin satirical journal, "Kladderadatsch", published a poem (see p. 48). It was easy for the Prussians to scoff – after all, it wasn't their King.

Ludwig, the Architect

ALL THE KING'S CASTLES

Ludwig II left us with three royal castles. To be more precise, he didn't actually leave them to us, the people that walk around in them today. After all they were not intended for us to "soil and desecrate" with our gazes. The King probably feels posthumously far more irritated than honoured by our presence; he would no doubt have preferred his castles to be blown up after his death.

Yet, on August 1st, 1886, very soon after the King's death, the castle gates were opened wide for the public, at the orders of the Prince-Regent Luitpold, his successor. It seemed that a long-held wish was now to be fulfilled.

Since that date guests from all corners of the globe have been coming to admire the King's castles: Some 1.4 million visit Neuschwanstein each year, 780,000 visit Linderhof, and a further 650,000 make the journey to Herrenchiemsee, and they are a real blessing to the region, to its guesthouse and café owners, car park owners, horse-drawn coach drivers, souvenir sellers, Chiemsee ship's captains, and to the reputation of Bavaria throughout the world.

No other Bavarian King has been as profitable as Ludwig II. Who would have thought it at the time?

In 1869 he began to build Linderhof Palace. In 1870 work began on Neuschwanstein Castle and in 1878 he laid the foundation stone for his Versailles palace on Chiemsee. His early death prevented the realisation of further, planned castle projects.

The Bavarian Royal Castles, here Linderhof Palace, are open throughout the year; in winter the numbers of visitors decline.

Les châteaux royaux bavarois – ici le château Linderhof – sont ouverts durant toute l'année; en hiver toutefois, rares sont les visiteurs.

I castelli reali bavaresi – qui il Castello di Linderhof – sono aperti tutto l'anno; a dire il vero d'inverno vengono pochi ospiti.

バイエルンの干城（写真はリンダーホーフ城）は年間を通して常に開いている。冬場にはむろん訪れる人は少ない。

Tours are offered in English and French, as well as in German.

Des visites guidées du château sont proposées en allemand, mais aussi en anglais et en français.

Visite guidate al castello sono disponibili non soltanto in tedesco, ma anche in inglese e francese.

ドイツ語はもちろん、英語・フランス語での城内ガイドも用意されている。

The castles were not intended as mere regal backdrops to grand court ceremonies and feasts, nor, as was the case with other monarchs before him, were they a means of securing a fitting place for their creator in the annals of history: Ludwig's castles were rather symbols of an ideal kingdom, images of mythical worlds from a glorious past, the embodiment of his dreams in splendidly ornate, gilded stone. They were his "joie de vivre", but also his sadness. For them he risked his freedom and his throne – and lost both.

He was obsessive and tireless in his passion for building. Countless Bavarian craftsmen were busily engaged in fulfilling their King's wishes, producing furniture and wall panels, weaving textiles, forging ornate door fittings, and turning chandeliers.

Everything else had to take second place to his building projects. No delays were tolerated. The painters worked day and night until they dropped, exhausted, from their ladders and scaffolding, and then they had to listen to a detailed catalogue of complaints and instructions on what they should do to improve their pictures. An oil painting in the lounge of Neuschwanstein Castle shows the legendary scene of Lohengrin's arrival in Antwerp. On seeing the original design

Herrenchiemsee was the most expensive of Ludwig's castles. The King spent 16.5 million gold marks on it up to 1885.

Herrenchiemsee fut le plus cher des châteaux de Louis. Jusqu'en 1885, le roi dépensa 16,5 millions de marks d'or pour ce château.

Herrenchiemsee fu il più costoso dei Castelli di Ludwig. Fino al 1885, per esso, il re spese 16,5 milioni di marchi-oro.

ヘレンキームゼーはルートヴィヒの王城のうち最も高価である。
1885年までに王は1650万金マルクをそのために費やしている。

View from Neuschwanstein to Hohenschwangau Castle, where the King used to spend many summers in his youth.

Vue à partir du Château de Neuschwanstein sur le château de Hohenschwangau dans lequel le jeune roi passa de nombreux étés.

Vista da Neuschwanstein sul castello di Hohenschwangau nel quale il re ha trascorso molte estati della sua giovinezza.

ノイシュヴァンシュタインからホーエンシュヴァンガウ城を望む。
この城で王は若き日の夏を幾度も過ごした。

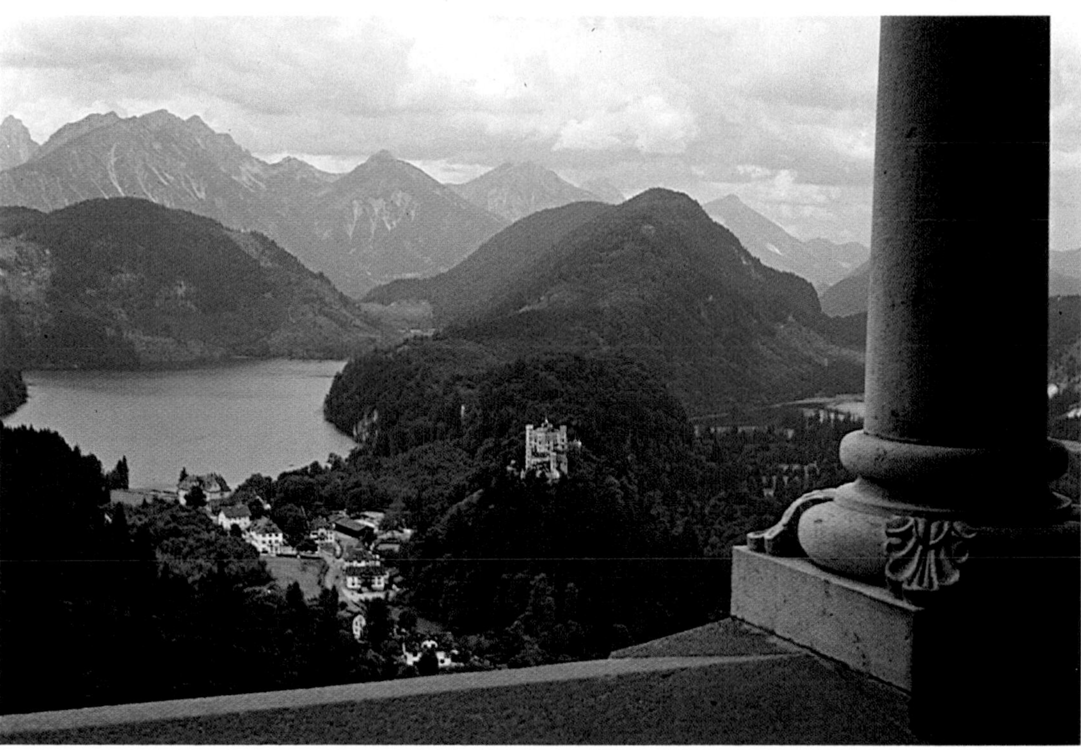

sketch the King let it be known to the artist that "His Majesty wishes that in the new sketch the ship should be further away from the banks, and that Lohengrin's head should not be tilted at such an angle; nor should the chain from the ship to the swan be made of roses, but of gold, and the castle should be in the mediaeval style." Or the artist in question would receive a letter from the King's confidant, Hornig, saying, for example, "Unfortunately the design for the door of the new bed chamber again did not meet with with His Highness's approval. As a correction His Majesty states: In general the design is not sufficiently rich. The rays of the sun are not painted finely enough. The face of the sun bears insufficient resemblance to that on the doors in Versailles, in particular the hair is not arranged as it is there. Around the sun is too much white, and in general it would look much richer if the relief decoration were carved in gold against a gold background…" – "In the former dining room His Majesty had expressly determined that Venus and Amor should be placed above the fireplace and that Venus and Bacchus should be placed above the window. Now the situation is exactly the reverse, which is most annoying for His Majesty, particularly as this can now no longer be changed."

Neuschwanstein is not a copy of another castle, but a completely new design by Ludwig and his architects.

Neuschwanstein n'est pas la copie d'un château existant, mais le fruit de l'imagination de Louis et de ses architectes.

Neuschwanstein non è la copia di un castello già esistente, ma una creazione personale di Ludwig e dei suoi architetti.

ノイシュヴァンシュタインは実存する城の模倣ではなく、ルートヴィヒと彼の建築家たち自身の創作である。

The King was in a great hurry. He would fly into a rage if work was delayed or if workers were unpunctual. Artists and craftsmen soon learned how quickly they could fall from grace. If they displeased, the King would write to his court secretary, saying: "Mr Zimmermann, the painter, promised to start the new picture immediately, and said that he would have it ready in 6 weeks. Now he is asking for 3 months in which to complete the work; Your Honourable King wishes therefore to take this work from him and give it to another, who would complete it equally well, in 6 weeks, this person being someone who could be relied upon not to produce slipshod work."

The King, as his sometimes dispairing craftsmen were to discover, was a very difficult customer to work for. It can hardly have been a very satisfying working relationship.

The three castles cost altogether 31 million marks, and today they bring in about 15 million per year in entrance monies.

They are open every day, but can only be viewed as part of a guided tour. On busy days some 6000, 8000 or even 10,000 or more visitors will be led sweating, panting and sniffing through the painstakingly conserved castle rooms, all the precious tapestries, curtains and carvings being safely cordoned off behind sturdy ropes. Precious items of furniture are surrounded, or "housed", as the jargon has it, in plexiglass cases, because so many of the guests simply cannot resist touching the objects; man is after all a very tactile animal and as such a natural enemy of works of art.

A guided tour lasts 20, 25 or 30 minutes and supplies the visiting crowds with detailed information on the history of the building and the artistic masterpieces that are gathered here, as well as inoffensive anecdotes and little details from the King's biography.

A figure of King Ludwig in tin, a popular souvenir produced in Diessen on the Ammersee.

Le roi Louis en tant que figurine de plomb, fabriquée à Diessen am Ammersee; un joli souvenir très apprécié.

Il Re Ludwig rappresentato come statuina di stagno, realizzato a Diessen am Ammersee, un souvenir popolare e grazioso.

ルートヴィヒ王の錫製の像。アンマー湖のそばのディーセンで作られた人気のある可愛らしい土産もの。

"This writing desk is a replica. The original is in Versailles. Fifteen different types of rare wood are inlaid into this desk. Over here we have an example of intarsia work. It is the most valuable piece in the whole castle." – "And these candelabras are genuine Meissen porcelain and today they are priceless. At the time they were made they cost around 80,000 gold marks." – "Those life-size peacocks are of Sèvres porcelain. There are two peacocks like this in the castle, and when the King was alive they were kept on the ground floor. When the King came to the castle, the peacocks were put at the entrance door, as a sign of his being in residence." – "Psychiatrists have said that the King was just as deranged as his brother. But this was not true – they only said it to get him away from the government more quickly."

Look at the King's nose for 30 seconds, then look at a light-coloured wall, and you will see the portrait of the King appear on the wall.

Si vous regardez durant 30 secondes le nez de Louis, puis contre un mur clair, le portrait du roi y apparaîtra.

Guardate per 30 secondi il naso di Ludwig, quindi rivolgete lo sguardo su una parete chiara: apparirà il ritratto del re.

このルートヴィヒの鼻を30秒間見つめて下さい。それから次に明るい色の壁を見て下さい。そこには王の肖像が現れるでしょう。

A souvenir of a plate, cup or beer mug is a ready reminder of your visit to the King's palaces.

Un souvenir, qu'il s'agisse d'une assiette, d'une tasse ou du pichet de mesure, rappelle inévitablement la visite chez le roi.

Un souvenir, che sia un piatto, una tazza o un boccale, ricorderà sempre la visita al re.

皿、カップやビールジョッキなどの土産ものは王のもとを訪れたことの確かな思い出となるでしょう。

The tour guides – eloquent people from the surrounding area (retired people, students, housewives) and staunch supporters of "their" King – also perform cleaning duties and work on the cash desks; they are given a basic text outline for the guided tour by the castles' administration authorities, but beyond that they are allowed a certain amount of freedom in how they present the tour. The pay is minimal, and, sadly, this does not seem to be supplemented too well by tips from the visitors. Murmuring a friendly "Auf Wiedersehen!" and "Have a nice day!", the guide stands next to the exit. "Thank you", "Grazie", "Pfiagood", "Bye Bye", "Au revoir" and "Sayonara" comes the visitors reply, but only a few feel occasioned to press a mark into the hand of their guide.

A tried and tested trick in such situations is to stand at the head of the queue of visitors on their way out of the castle, and loudly proclaim "Oh, thank you very much!", so that the ones further back in the queue can hear and have sufficient time to produce an appropriate tip. However, this method is viewed as rather unrefined and frowned upon by the castles' administration authorities.

Linderhof

A Modest Palace

In Graswang valley, near to Garmisch-Partenkirchen, the Ettal Monastery and the village of Oberammergau, King Maximilian II had one of his secluded hunting lodges, a little wooden refuge known as the "King's hut". Here, in 1868/69 Ludwig decided three things. Firstly, this was to be the place for a "new Versailles"; or secondly, perhaps it would be more suited for a "Byzantine palace"; but thirdly, possibly a "royal villa", made up of a "small pavilion" and a "not too large garden in the Renaissance style", everything was to be of "rather modest dimensions". For himself, the King noted, he needed "only three, somewhat more richly decorated and elegantly furnished rooms".

New Versailles was constructed at a later date on an island in Lake Chiemsee. The Byzantine palace was never built. The third plan – for the "royal villa" – was the one to be carried out at Linderhof. Yet the finished version, when the King finally moved in, bore little resemblance to a modest villa. The King had underestimated his requirements: no sooner had the study, bed chamber and dining room been added to the "King's hut", than the wooden hut was torn down to make way for a more substantial stone construction with a staircase. More rooms were added on the first floor, and the size of the King's bed chamber grew and grew: every couple of years he had it extended.

Finally, in 1878, the building was at last finished; what was originally planned as a modest "villa" had become a splendid Rococo palace in the ornate French style.

Visitors are most interested in the

Linderhof, the smallest of the three royal castles, and the only one which was completely finished (1878).

Linderhof, le plus petit des trois châteaux royaux et le seul réellement achevé (en 1878).

Linderhof, il più piccolo dei tre castelli reali e l'unico che fu effettivamente finito (1878).

リンダーホーフ城。3つの王城の中で一番小さく、そして唯一（1878年に）実際に完成した城。

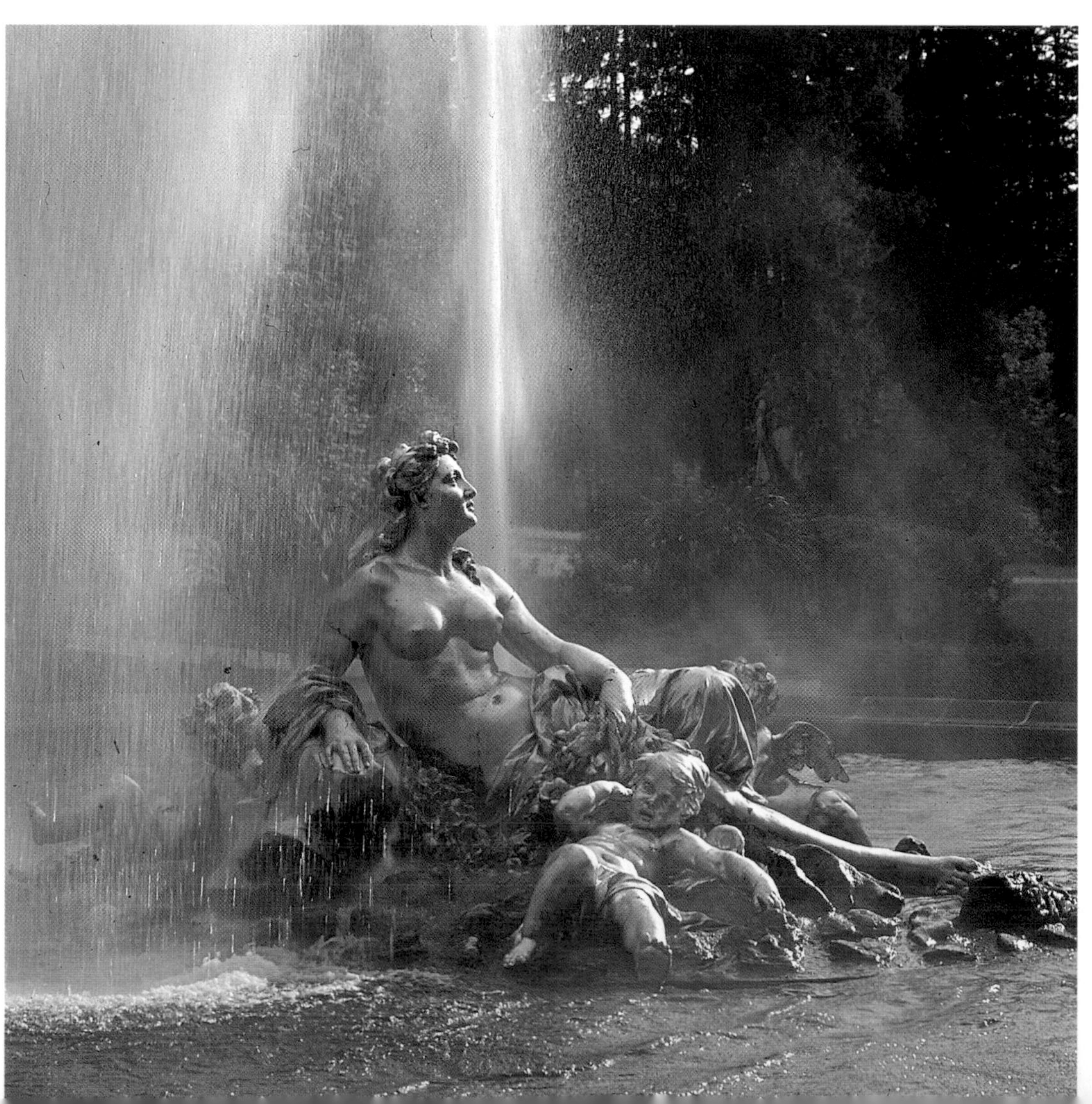

Gilded statue with fountain in the French garden, on the edge of 500,000 square metres of English-style parkland.

Statue dorée avec fontaine dans le Jardin Français qui mène au Parc Anglais d'une superficie de 500.000 m^2.

Statua dorata con fontana nel giardino francese che si muta in un parco all'inglese di 500.000 m^2.

フランス庭園の噴水の中の金メッキの像。この庭園は50万平米のイギリス庭園へと続いている。

A fairytale "magic" table which disappears into the floor. Ludwig had one installed in both Herrenchiemsee and here in Linderhof.

Louis possédait une « table couvre-toi » qui disparaissait dans le sol tant à Herrenchiemsee qu'ici, à Linderhof.

Un «tavolo magico», che sparisce nel pavimento, Ludwig lo aveva sia a Herrenchiemsee che a Linderhof.

「魔法の食卓」。床下に隠れる。ルートヴィヒはここリンダーホーフの他、ヘレンキームゼー城にも同じものを持っていた。

The royal bed chamber in Linderhof: a giant-sized bed for a larger-than-life King. Ludwig particularly liked ornate drapes in his bedroom.

Chambre à coucher à Linderhof avec lit immense pour un roi immense. Louis attachait une importance particulière aux chambres à coucher empreintes de magnificence.

Camera da letto a Linderhof col letto gigantesco per un re gigantesco. Ludwig attribuì sempre particolare valore a camere da letto ampollose.

巨体の王のための巨大なベッドのあるリンダーホーフの寝室。
きらびやかな寝室にルートヴィヒは常に桁外れの貴重品を置いていた。

The Germanic Hunding Hut in the grounds of Linderhof Palace. It is a copy of the one used in the stage set for the premiere of the Valkyries.

La hutte germanique Hunding dans le parc du château Linderhof; construite d'après de décor d'opéra de la première de la Walkyrie.

La capanna germanica di Hunding nel parco del Castello di Linderhof, costruita sul modello della scenografia della prima delle Valchirie.

リンダーホーフ城の庭園のゲルマン風のフンディング小屋。
ヴァルキューレの初演の舞台画に基づいて造られた。

King's bed chamber ("Here we can see the King's bed, two metres 60 long, 2.49 metres wide.") and the hall of mirrors ("If you stand here it seems as if you are in an endless corridor."), but also, in particular, in the dining room. For here, and in Herrenchiemsee Palace, they can see something straight from the pages of a Grimm's fairy story: a magic dining table which sinks through the floor (the opening then closes up) to the kitchens below, where it is decked with food and sent back up to the dining room. The advantage of this technology was that the King did not have to see his servants. "The mechanism is still operational, but we don't do demonstrations any more", we learn from the guide, to our great dismay. Yet this really would not be practicable; apart from the fact that a demonstration every ten minutes would soon lead to a total breakdown, it is in fact quite a difficult operation to perform. This latter problem, of course, did not trouble the King in the least.

The tour inside the palace lasts about twenty minutes, and then the visitors are taken into the castle grounds to see the grotto. "This is something really special", says the guide, "for everything that you see here is artificial. The whole grotto consists of a giant iron framework which was filled in with cement and shell limestone to make it seem natural."

The visitor listens attentively, but his inquisitive nature compels him to test the

The "Moorish Kiosk", acquired by Ludwig in 1876 for the gardens of Linderhof Palace. This kiosk had originally been designed for the World Exhibition in Paris in 1867.

Le « Kiosque Mauresque » dans le parc de Linderhof. En 1876, Louis l'acheta à un constructeur de chemins de fer qui avait fait faillite.

Il «chiosco moresco» nel parco di Linderhof. Ludwig lo acquistò nel 1876 da un costruttore di ferrovie fallito.

リンダーホーフの庭園内の「ムーア風キオスク」。
1876年にルートヴィヒが倒産した鉄道建設業主から買い取ったもの。

truth of this statement, and so he crooks the fingers of his hand and taps against the rock wall as he passes. Its hollow ring confirms that it is artificial. If we assume that, apart from a very small number of disinterested people, every visitor taps three times with a force of 150 grams per tap, then we can calculate that the rock wall has to withstand a total 350,000 kilograms of test taps in the course of a single year, and in three years this figure can reach as much as one megaton. The fact that it is nevertheless still standing is proof that it is a masterpiece of grotto craftsmanship.

Also artificial, but with real water, is the lake in the grotto; it reaches a depth of three metres and is even equipped with a wave-making machine. Originally it was to be intended to be used for staging performances of Wagner operas, where it would be used as the landing place for Lohengrin, the swan knight, and as the pool in which the Rhine Maidens frolicked. Sadly, the acoustics were not suitable for opera and so no performances were held here. Instead the King used to have his servants row him across the cave in a golden shell-shaped boat; when the lighting was switched to red he would imagine he were in the mountain cave of the lovely Venus; with blue lighting it became the grotto of Capri.

Further afield in the gardens of the castle the visitor can marvel at an oriental curiosity – the "Moorish Kiosk", and before leaving the grounds he can pay a visit to Hunding's Hut, where the King used to spend his time when he was in a particularly Germanic frame of mind.

Wagner fans will already know what Hunding's Hut is. It features in the first act of the Valkyries, where Siegmund snatches his beloved twin sister, Sieglinde, together with the mighty sword, Nothung, from the treacherous Hunding. Ludwig had the hut built in 1876, but in 1945 it was destroyed in an arson attack. In 1990 it was rebuilt and opened again to the public.

It was here on the banks of a small pond in this log cabin built around a beech tree disguised as an ash that Ludwig used to lounge on furs in front of an open fire. Here, we read on a notice on the wall of the hut, he "used to spend moonlit nights reading and meditating. The oversized drinking horns would seem to indicate, however, that pleasures of a quite different sort were also part of these atmospheric evenings around the fire, when the Linderhof stable hands and servants would lounge on bearskins, quaffing mead, acting out Ludwig's Germanic fantasies".

The centrepiece of the "Moorish Kiosk" is the peacock's throne (right), a divan surrounded by three peacocks.

La pièce maîtresse du « Kiosque Mauresque » est le « Trône des Paons » (à droite): un divan entouré de trois paons.

Il pezzo forte del «Chiosco moresco» è il «trono dei pavoni» (a destra): un divano circondato da tre pavoni.

「ムーア風キオスク」の見もの、「孔雀の玉座」（右）：
３羽の孔雀に囲まれた寝椅子。

Neuschwanstein Castle

PROUD, NOBLE TOWERS

The most famous of Ludwig's castles and the most prized by the visitors is Neuschwanstein. Built in Romanesque style, "the true style of German knights' castles", it gleams snow-white atop a steep cliff against a picturesque background of high mountains; it looks the very image of a fairytale castle for a legendary King. The King who created it, however, was not at home very often – Ludwig lived here for a total of only 172 days.

The construction of the castle lasted from 1869 to 1886. The chosen location was "the place where once the two castles of Vorderhohenschwangau and Hinterhohenschwangau had raised their crenellated parapets". – "This new castle will in every respect be much more beautiful and habitable than the lower Hohenschwangau Castle which is desecrated annually by the prosaic presence of my mother", Ludwig once wrote to Wagner.

Neuschwanstein is Germany's most-visited castle and most-photographed building, and it is even more famous than Versailles. This castle appears more frequently than any other on beer mugs, T-shirts, walking sticks, ashtrays, plates and cups. Every American tourist knows of it, if only from its copy in Disneyland. The real Neuschwanstein draws 1.3 million visitors every year.

On busy summer weekends there can be up to 12,000 visitors on a single day; they wait two hours, or even three, slowly and patiently inching their way up the narrow staircase towards the entrance on the second floor where they join one of the two queues. On the left are visitors from Japan, China, France or the USA and on the right wait the Germans.

A notice informs them that the German tour takes place every 20 minutes, the English one every 25 minutes and the French tour every 25 minutes. The wrought iron gates, carefully guarded by the gatekeeper, are still closed, but soon they will open up. A small child at the back of the queue gets into trouble with his grandparents; he doesn't want to go and see the King, but he'll just have to do as they say and go along.

At the front, at the head of the German queue, people start to move. The iron gates open, letting in a maximum of 60 visitors at a time.

A young woman welcomes us and explains with regret that Neuschwanstein Castle (which in King Ludwig's day was still called the "New Hohenschwangau Castle") is only one third complete, despite 17 years of intensive building work which went into it.

It wasn't exactly 17 years, however, but slightly more, because work was not stopped completely after the King's death; urgent structural work still had to be finished. Between 1868 and 1892 the décor and furnishing of the interior rooms was completed "and the external appearance of the ladies' apartments and the knights' quarters (the 'Ritterbau') were finished so as to give the whole complex a unified, overall impression, albeit somewhat sobre due to the lack of architectural sculpture on the outside". Sadly, plans for a castle keep, (the tall tower on the left-hand side of the design sketch on page 38/39) which was to have towered above the whole palatial ensemble, had to be abandoned – if it had been built it would have been a very fitting addition to the whole fairytale image of Neuschwanstein.

The guide informs us that the castle was built in the style of late Romanesque castles of the Hohenstaufen dynasty, or at least the 19th century visions of that era

**Previous double page:
The Forggensee, south of Füssen, with a view of Neuschwanstein Castle. This lake is a reservoir and only holds water in summer.**

**Page double précédente:
Le Forggensee au sud de Füssen, avec vue sur le château de Neuschwanstein. Il s'agit d'un lac avec barrage qui est rempli d'eau uniquement en été.**

**Doppia pagina precedente:
Il lago Forggensee a sud di Füssen, con vista sul castello di Neuschwanstein. E' un lago artificiale e contiene acqua solo d'estate.**

前ページ見開き：
フュッセンの南方にあるフォーゲン湖。ノイシュヴァンシュタイン城が見える。ここは貯水湖で夏期のみ水をたたえている。

Neuschwanstein – seen here from the south – stands 1008 metres above sea level and 200 m high on a cliff above the valley.

Neuschwanstein – vu du sud – est situé à 1008 mètres au-dessus du niveau de la mer et à 200 mètres au-dessus de la vallée, sur un rocher.

Neuschwanstein – qui visto da sud – è sito su un picco a 1008 metri sul livello del mare e a 200 metri sulla valle.

写真は南側から見たノイシュヴァンシュタイン。海抜1008メータ、谷から200メータの高さの岩塊の上にそびえる。

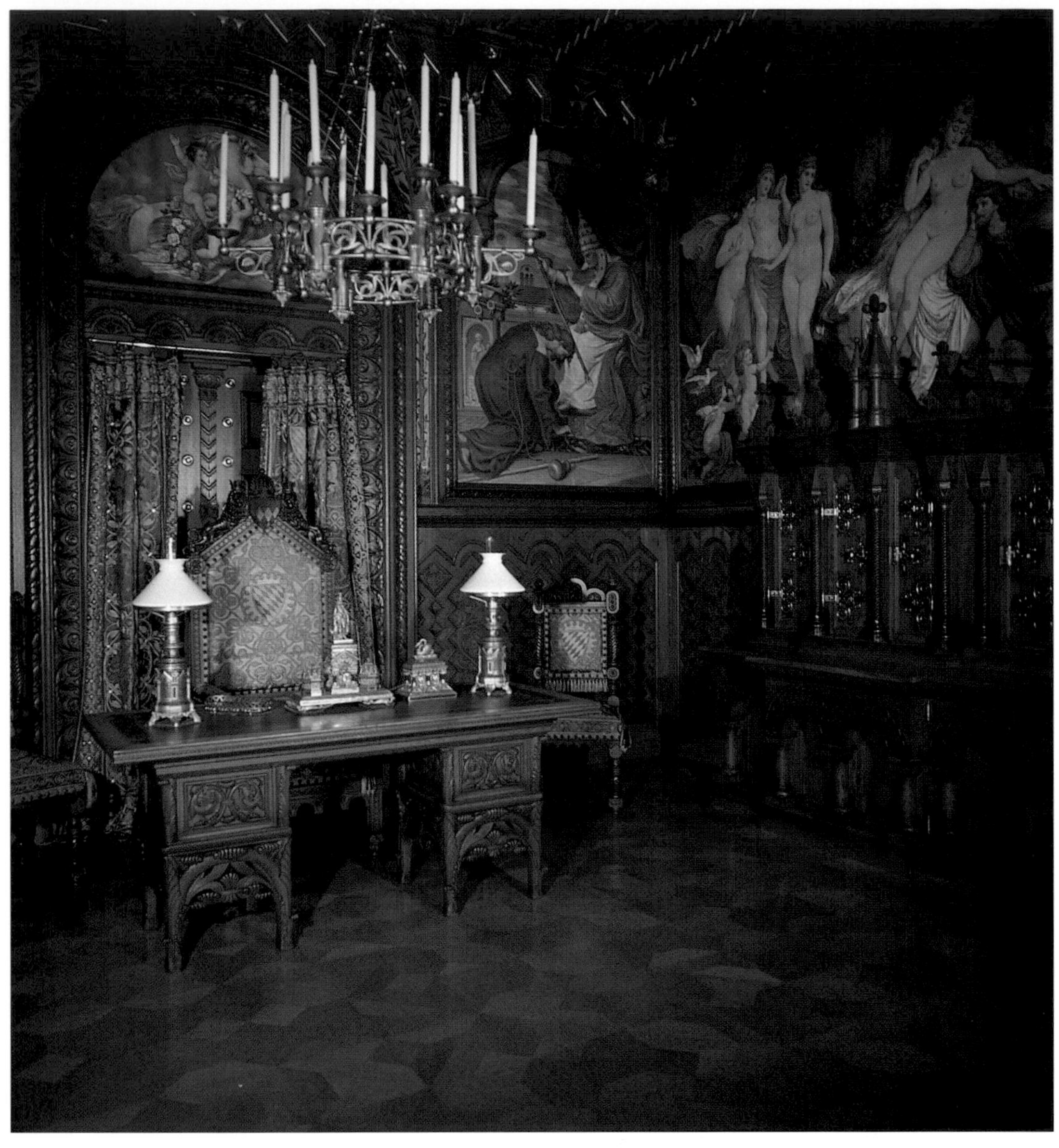

The King's study on the third floor of Neuschwanstein Castle. The walls are painted with scenes from Tannhäuser.

La salle de travail royale au troisième étage du château de Neuschwanstein avec les peintures murales de Tannhäuser.

Lo studio reale al terzo piano del castello di Neuschwanstein con pitture murali raffiguranti Tannhäuser.

ノイシュヴァンシュタイン城の3階にある王の書斎。タンホイザーの壁画がある。

as held by King Ludwig and his theatre set designer, Christian Jank: "Just as they used to build in days of old."

We pass hurriedly through servants dormitories, and have to climb 63 steps up to the solemn and ceremonial Throne Room. Byzantine style, we hear, mosaic flooring with ornamental designs and plant and animal motifs, paintings on 24-carat gold leaf and a most interesting picture of the saintly dragon-killer, George, with Falkenstein Castle in the background. This castle is worthy of particular note, as it does not in fact exist – the King had intended it as one of his next castle projects, but it was not to be. Rows of columns and arcaded walks surround the hall. Angels, law-makers, apostles and six canonised kings look benignly down upon us from the walls.

"The chandelier in the shape of a Byzantine crown weighs one ton." Carefully we walk past, not underneath but skirting around it. Marble steps lead up to the throne apse, but the King never sat on his throne here; the reason was that the royal

The Throne Room (illustrated) and the Minstrels' Hall are the two main attractions in Neuschwanstein Castle.

La Salle du Trône (sur la photographie) et la Salle des Chanteurs sont les pièces maîtresses du château de Neuschwanstein.

La sala del trono (nella foto) la sala dei cantori rappresentano il cuore del castello di Neuschwanstein.

玉座の間（写真）と歌人の広間はノイシュヴァンシュタイン城の中心的存在である。

An example of master craftsmanship: filigree wrought iron work on the door of the King's dressing room.

Œuvres artisanales réalisées avec une grande maîtrise. Ferrure de porte du salon d'habillage.

Artigianato d'autore. Guarnizione metallica di porte dello spogliatoio.

見事な工芸品、化粧室のドア金具。

throne of gold and ivory was never actually delivered. The next two rooms are servants' quarters, then comes the royal bed chamber in late Gothic style. The baldachine took 14 master craftsmen four and a half years to carve.

We stand a while in the royal lounge and look in amazement at the dozen or so wall paintings of Lohengrin, Elsa von Brabant and also the swan, the King's favourite bird, which is depicted on countless cushions, drapes and table cloths. We enter a grotto with artificial stalagmites and stalactites, smaller than Linderhof, but here, too, we learn, there is also a choice of lighting – either pink or blue. Originally the grotto not only had a golden moon but also a waterfall; unfortunately the water has been turned off. The King also conceived the idea of having a waterfall tumbling down one of the flights of stairs at the castle, but he was finally persuaded by his worried advisors, fearing major flooding, that this was possibly an unwise scheme. Passing through the grotto we reach the King's study, dedicated to Richard Wagner's "Tannhäuser".

Moorish influences at Neuschwanstein are quite modest; in the winter garden is a Turkish fountain; a Moorish hall was planned but never carried out.

Once again upwards, 32 steps to the fourth floor, to the Minstrels' Hall, modelled on the hall at Wartburg Castle, where the legendary song contest was held. Beautiful paintings showing scenes from Parsifal decorate the walls of this splendid hall.

"The setting and the interiors are exceptionally beautiful and can only call forth admiration in even the most hardened critic", wrote the author of an 1894

Court life never filled these splendid castles. Only the King promenaded dreamily through the empty halls.

La vie de la cour n'a jamais animé les splendides châteaux; seul le roi solitaire déambulait au fil de ses rêves.

La vita di corte non regnò mai nei sontuosi castelli, soltanto il re solitario passeggiava in essi inseguendo i suoi sogni.

華やかな城では宮廷風の生活はついに送られることがなく、孤独な王がここで散さくし、夢想に耽るのみであった。

travel guide. So let us also not waste our energies in casting allegations of "Historicism!" or "Kitsch!", but let us instead turn to the question which most concerns the castle visitors: What did Neuschwanstein Castle cost? – 6.2 million marks.

And how much does it bring in each year? – 7.8 millions.

These are figures which would indeed warm the heart of any estate agent; even if we apply complicated multiplications to 19th century prices to enable a true comparison with today's price levels, the balance sheet could hardly look more favourable.

The castles' administration authorities, of course, do not share this opinion and are at pains to stress that the financial realities of the situation are a little different, pointing out that the entrance monies from Neuschwanstein are not reserved exclusively for this castle, but flow into more general state coffers. However, if we nevertheless view Neuschwanstein in isolation, and leave aside the question of initial capital investment, site value and the building costs, "then Neuschwanstein is, as it were, a winner", its income does indeed exceed expenditure, but only just, because costs for personnel

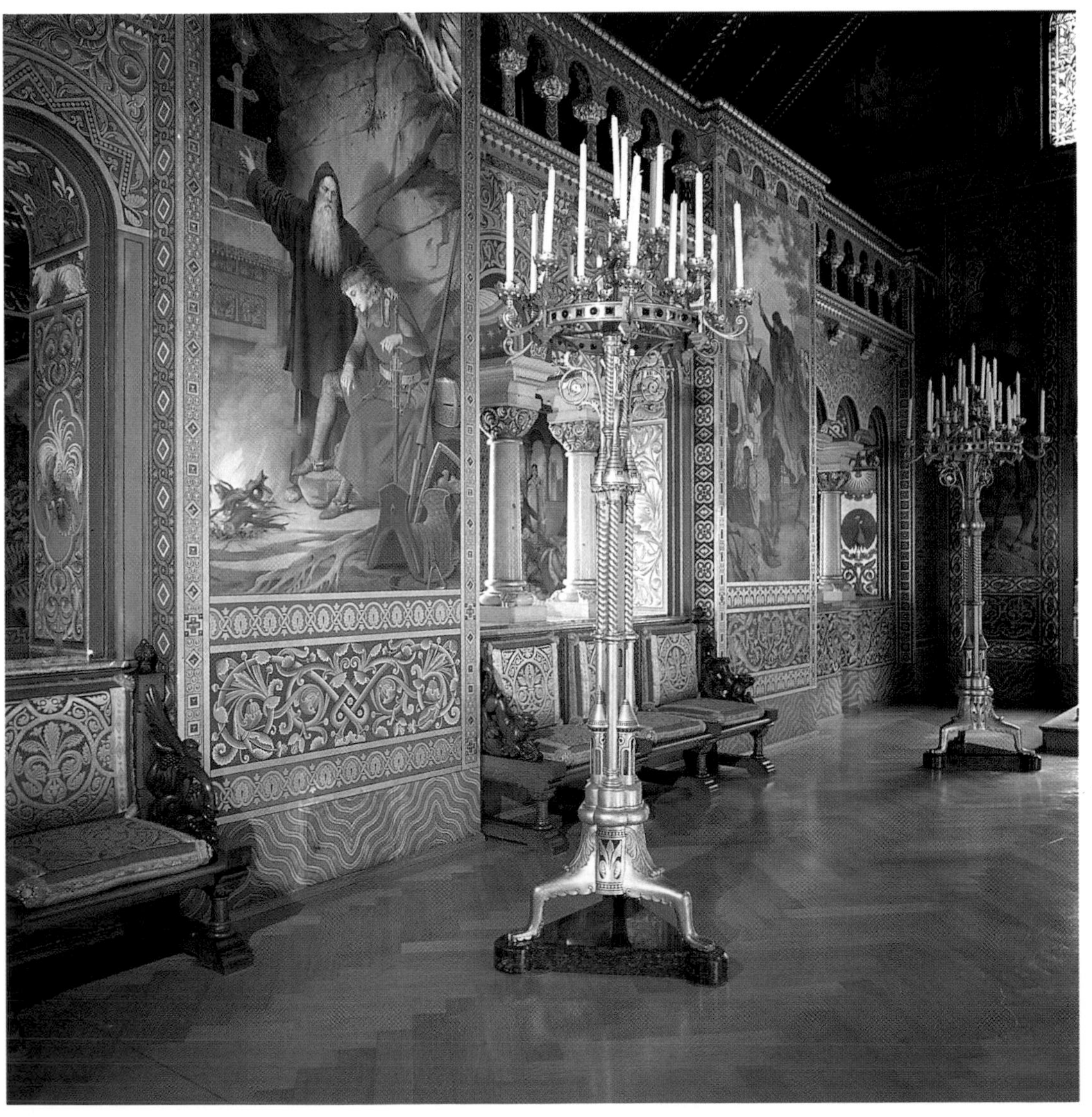

Scenes from the Parsifal legend are depicted on the wall paintings in the Minstrels' Hall.

Les tableaux muraux de la Salle des Chanteurs nous présentent des scènes extraites de la légende de Parsifal.

I dipinti murali della sala dei cantori ci presentano scene dalla leggenda di Parsifal.

歌人の広間の壁画は我々をパルツィファルの伝説のシーンへと誘う。

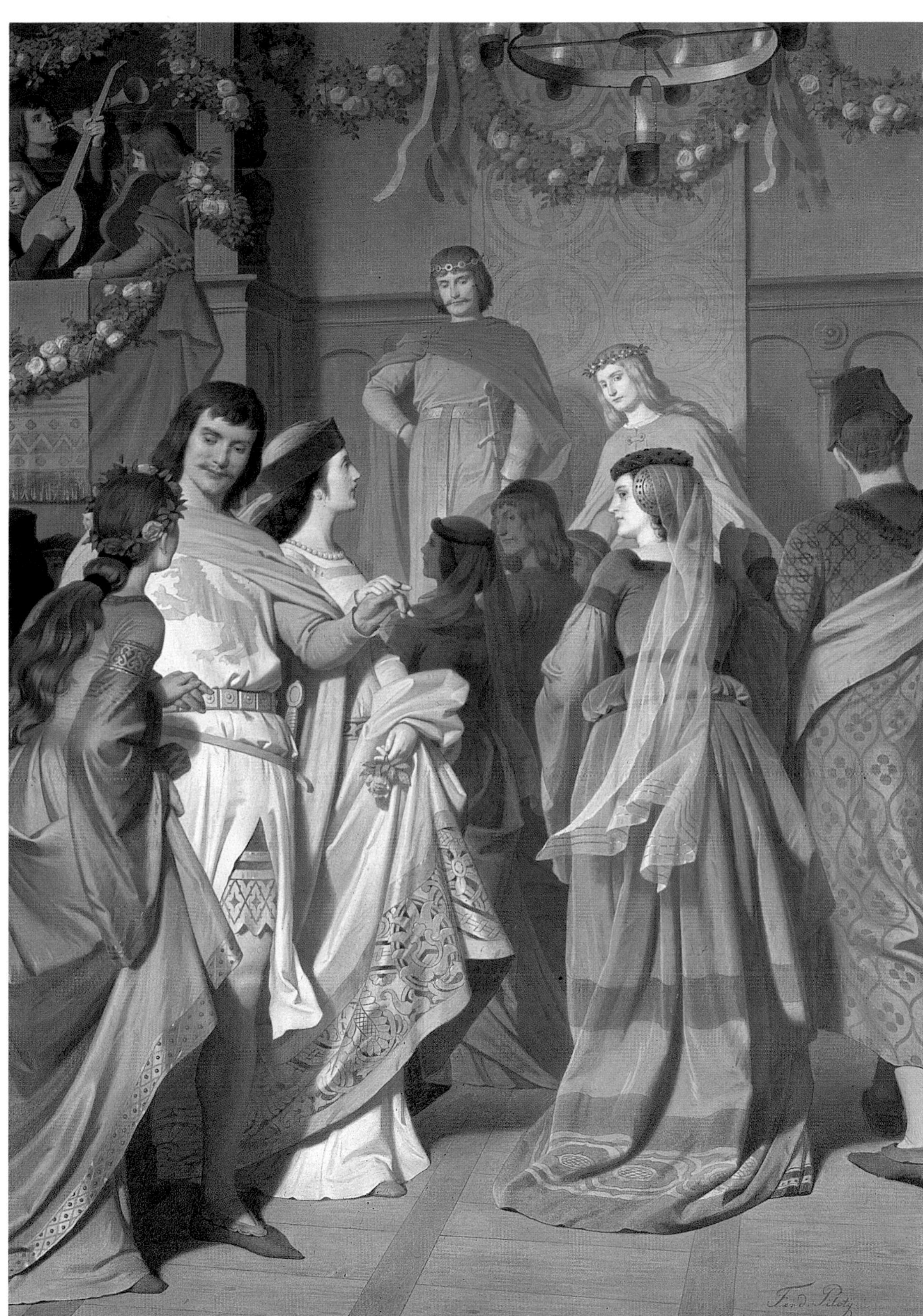

Fresco in the singer's arbour in the Minstrels' Hall.

Fresque de la tribune de la Salle des Chanteurs. Elle montre « La célébration du mariage de Gawan avec Orgelusen ».

Affresco nel corridoio delle tribune della sala dei cantori. Mostra le «Nozze di Gawan con Orgelusen».

歌人の広間の観覧席のフレスコ画。「ガヴァンの婚礼とオーゲルーゼン」を示している。

American tourists are already familiar with Neuschwanstein; the "Sleeping Beauty Castle" in Disneyland was modelled on it.

Les touristes américains connaissent Neuschwanstein de leur patrie où il est représenté à Disneyland en tant que « Sleeping Beauty Castle ».

I turisti americani conoscono già dalla loro patria il castello di Neuschwanstein, il cui modello si erge a Disneyland col nome di «Castello della Bella Addormentata».

アメリカ人の旅行者は自国のノイシュヴァンシタインを知っている。
それはディズニーランドの眠れる森の美女の城である。

and building conservation are enormously high, as the following example will illustrate: "In 1977 major construction work had to be carried out to strengthen the cliff foundations below the ladies' apartments, at a cost of half a million Deutschmarks. The costs for renovating the Marienbrücke over Pöllat's Gorge amounted to approximately DM 640,000. A further 2.1 million Deutschmarks were spent on new copper roofing for the castle. Restoration work on the furniture and fittings at the castle is an on-going process and money has to be invested in fire safety measures and in improving the guided tours for the visitors. A new visitors entrance was created by sinking a stairwell and boring a tunnel through the cliff. To date the Bavarian castles' and palaces' administration authorities has spent about DM 5.8 million on necessary building work. Work still to be done is estimated at DM 7 million." All this goes to show: even a successful King Ludwig castle has its fair share of problems – as the King himself discovered, when he was the owner.

King Ludwig, not about to engage in a swordfight, but playing the role of Grand Master of the Order of the Knights of Saint George.

Le roi Louis, non pas dans un duel d'épée, mais en tant que grand maître de l'Ordre des Chevaliers de Saint Georges.

Il Re Ludwig, che non è rappresentato mentre si accinge a un duello con la spada, bensì in veste di Gran Maestro dell'Ordine dei Cavalieri di San Giorgio.

ルートヴィヒ王。剣の決闘の際というよりは聖なるゲオルクの騎士団の大将として。

Previous double page: Herrenchiemsee Palace. In the background is the tiny island of Krautinsel, and, behind it, the idyllic Fraueninsel with its mighty church tower.

Page double précédente: Château Herrenchiemsee. En arrière-plan, la petite Krautinsel et l'idyllique Fraueninsel avec la tour imposante de son cloître.

Doppia pagina precedente: Castello di Herrenchiemsee. Sullo sfondo la piccola Krautinsel e l'idillica Fraueninsel con l'imponente torrione del chiostro.

前ページ見開き：
ヘレンキームゼー城。背景には小さなクラウト島と、重厚な修道院の塔のある牧歌的なフラウエン島が見える。

650,000 visitors come to Herrenchiemsee Palace each year.

650.000 visiteurs se rendent chaque année au Château Herrenchiemsse.

650.000 visitatori si recano ogni anno al castello di Herrenchiemsee.

ヘレンキームゼー城には年間65万人もが訪れる。

The splendid staircase in Herrenchiemsee, inspired by the Ambassadors Staircase in Versailles.

La montée d'escalier fastueuse de Herrenchiemsee; une copie de l'Escalier des Envoyés de Versailles.

Lo sfarzoso scalone di Herrenchiemsee, copia dello scalone degli Ambasciatori di Versailles.

ヘレンキームゼーの豪華な階段。ヴェルサイユ宮殿の公使階段の模倣。

Herrenchiemsee

A PALACE FOR TEN DAYS

To reach Herrenchiemsee you take the Salzburg autobahn as far as the Bernau exit and then head for Stock, near Prien, a journey of about 90 kilometres from Munich. From Stock a 15-minute boat trip takes you across the Chiemsee to the island of Herreninsel. Then a short walk uphill to the Palace Hotel, through the beer garden, past the ruins of a church and along a path through fields and woods to Ludwig's final castle, and the biggest and most expensive of all at 16.6 million. It looks like Versailles, or at least half of Versailles. The wings are missing, the right-hand one was never built and the shell of the other one was torn down in 1907.

Guides accompany the visitors, in groups of 80, through the vestibule, the staircase and the "Hartschier Saal", a hall which takes its name from the King's bodyguard, the Hartschier Halbardiers. Beyond that is the first ante-room, then the second ante-room, and finally the royal bed chamber in which no-one ever slept. It was intended more as a monu-

ment to Louis XIV and is a copy of the chamber in which the Bourbons used to hold the first and last audiences of the day. Thirty industrious women, we hear, worked for 7 years on the embroidery for the bed cover. The palace has 70 rooms, of which 50 were never completed. There is no electric light, only a few sockets for the vacuum cleaners. In 1873 the King purchased the island to save its trees from being felled, and in 1878 the foundation stone for the palace was laid. Ludwig lived here for a total of just 10 days, in September 1885.

The most famous part of the palace is the Hall of Mirrors. The guide informs us that it is 98 metres long, and has 44 candelabras and 33 chandeliers; candle-lit concerts used to be held here, but they were discontinued because the smoke caused discolouration of the ceiling.

"Gilt work is everywhere in the palace, yet only four and a half kilos of 22-carat gold were used." – "Only?" – "Yes, it's quite a small amount really."

What we see and admire here is not great art, but rather perfect examples of master craftsmanship, and, as in Ludwig's other castles, we are entranced less by their exquisite beauty than the fantastic, effusive splendour they embody.

A heavily ornate baldachine surrounds the almost two-and-a-half-metres long royal bed which is sectioned off from the rest of the room by a golden balustrade.

The 98-metres long Hall of Mirrors in Herrenchiemsee is longer than the one in Versailles.

La Salle des Glaces de Herrenchiemsee dépasse son modèle versaillais avec 98 mètres de longueur.

Il salone degli specchi di Herrenchiemsee, con i suoi 98 metri, supera la lunghezza del suo modello di Versailles.

ヘレンキームゼーの鏡の間は奥行き98
で、手本となったヴェルサイユのそれを上回る。

Only six weeks after Ludwig's death the doors of his castles were open to the people.

Les châteaux royaux ont été ouverts au public pour des visites six semaines seulement après la mort de Louis.

Dopo sole sei settimane dalla morte di Ludwig i castelli reali furono aperta alla visita del pubblico.

ルートヴィヒの死の6週間後には既に王城は一般の見学に公開された。

In front of this balustrade is a gilt stand with golden puttos lazily entwined around a stem supporting a large blue glass ball. "This ball" we are told, "is a light. In it burned a flame which bathed the room in blue light. Blue, royal blue, was the King's favourite colour."

Steps lead down from the dressing room to the ground floor; here were the royal kitchens and Ludwig's round, marble, heated swimming pool which measures seven and a half metres across and one metre seventy deep. "The King was never able to use it, because until his death this palace was a building site."

The tour lasts 35 minutes. Then the visitor has the opportunity of looking around the King Ludwig II Museum.

A 20-minute walk or a short trip in a horse and carriage takes visitors from the jetty to the palace.

Un chemin pédestre de 20 minutes, mais aussi des calèches relient les embarcadères et le château.

L'imbarcadero è collegato al castello non solo da una camminata di 20 minuti per il sentiero, ma anche da carrozze a cavalli.

歩くと20分の歩道を通る以外に、馬車が船着場と城を連結している。

The majestic splendour of the audience hall in Herrenchiemsee. The wall painting is of Louis XIV.

La somptueuse Salle du Conseil à Herrenchiemsee. Le tableau mural montre Louis XIV.

La sfarzosa sala delle udienze a Herrenchiemsee. Il dipinto alla parete mostra Luigi XIV.

ヘレンキームゼー城の会議室。壁画はルイXIV世。

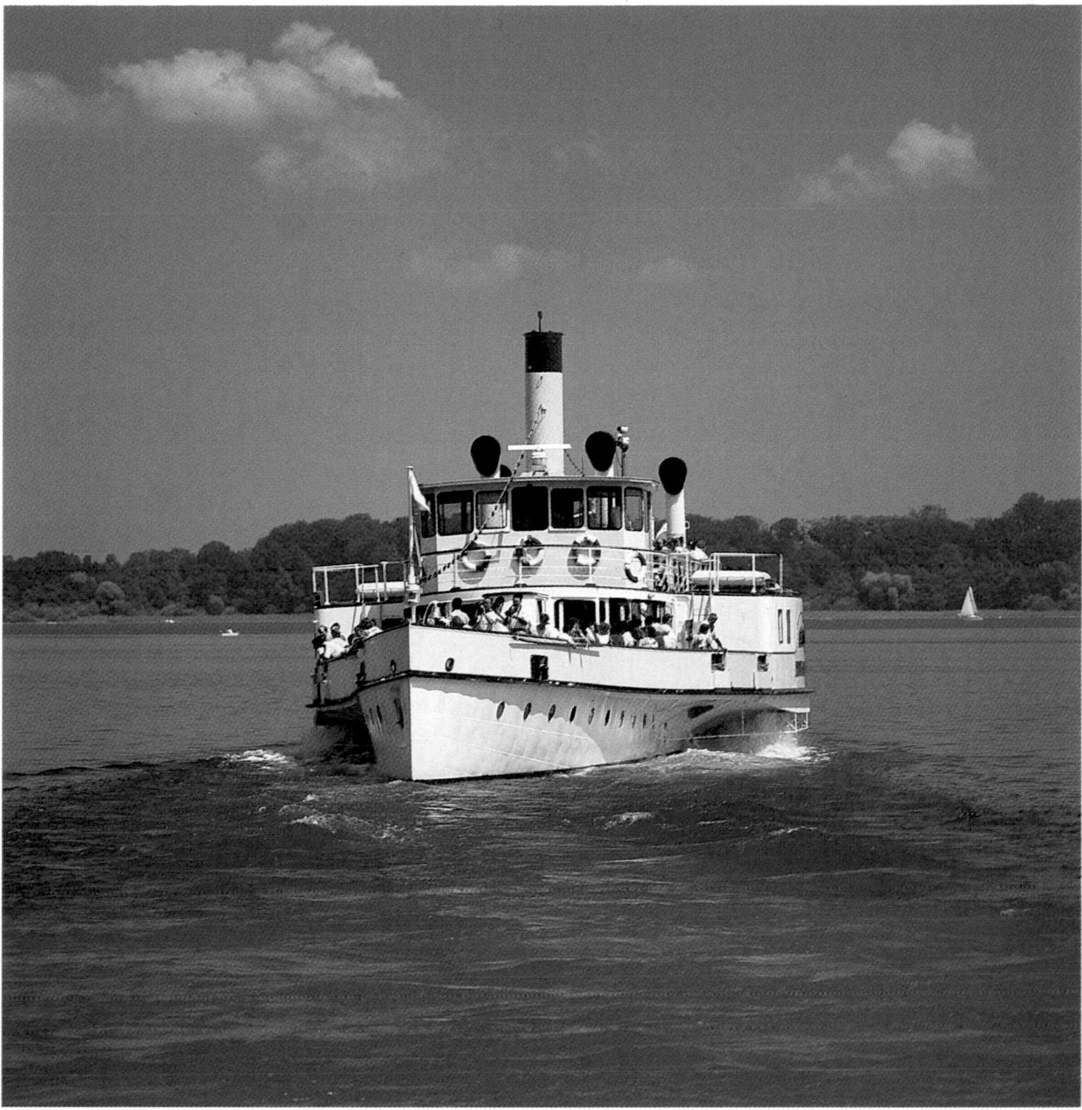

The trip on the Chiemsee steamer from Prien to Herrenchiemsee Island takes a quarter of an hour.

La promenade en bateau d'excursion Chiemsee de Prien jusqu'à l'île Herrenchiemsee dure un quart d'heure.

Il tragitto sulla barca turistica dello Chiemsee, da Prien all'isola di Herrenchiemsee, dura un quarto d'ora.

キームゼー遊覧船でプリーンからヘレン島までの所要時間は15分。

In this museum is Ludwig's christening gown, busts of the King and his brother as children, the royal Bavarian coronation robes and various items of furniture, paintings from his apartments in the Residence Palace, and models and plans for his uncompleted castle projects. Here, too, is his death mask and a plaster cast of one hand. Notices give snippets of biographical information: "Signs of chronic distrust and extreme irritation appeared", "Excessive indulgence in sweets ruined his teeth", and on another we read that while she was engaged to Ludwig, his intended bride, Sophie, is supposed to have had "an illicit romance" with the son of the court photographer.

The King even tried his hand at poetry, albeit with modest success. When his friend, the Empress Elisabeth of Austria, wrote him a letter in rhyme, he courteously penned the following note of thanks:

"Der Möwe Gruß vom fernen Strand
zu Adlers Horst den Weg wohl fand.
Er trug auf leisem Fittigschwung
der alten Zeit Erinnerung."

"From far-flung shores the seagull's greeting
To the eagle's nest its way did find.
Bearing with it on soft flitting wing,
Sweet memories of old times."

The King drove in his coach to the Hunting Lodge on the Schachen. Today's visitors are obliged to walk.

Le roi se rendait en calèche à son pavillon de chasse de Schachen. Les visiteurs doivent monter aujourd'hui à pied.

Il re si recava in carrozza al suo castello di caccia di Schachen. I visitatori odierni devono salire a piedi.

狩猟城シャッヘンへ馬車で行く王。今日訪れる人は徒歩で登らなければならない。

The King did not use his Hunting Lodge as a base for hunting expeditions, but instead as a "blissful retreat".

Le roi employait son pavillon de chasse de Schachen non seulement pour la chasse, mais aussi pour se retirer dans une « douce solitude ».

Il re non usava il suo castello di Schachen per andare a caccia, ma per ritirarsi in «deliziosa solitudine».

王は狩猟のためではなく、「快い孤独」に浸るために狩猟城シャッヘンを利用した。

The Hunting Lodge on the Schachen

CALIPH LUDWIG

People like things easy: 1.3 million visitors find their way each year to Neuschwanstein, but a mere 6,700 get as far as the Royal Hunting Lodge on the Schachen. Not because the tourists do not like it, nor because they are not interested, but because it is situated 1866 metres high up on a mountain, with no railway, no chair lift and no public road. The only way to get there is to walk for three, four, or five hours uphill from Garmisch-Partenkirchen or Elmau. Confronted with this level of effort, even the fittest King Ludwig fans think twice about the necessity of seeing all of his buildings, and content themselves instead with the ones in less strenuous locations.

Sports fanatics may even make the journey on mountain bikes, but this is rather frowned upon because of the environmental damage caused by their thick tyres; the foresters and administrators of the castles' authorities cover the stretch in sturdy four-wheel drive vehicles, a trip of about an hour over very bumpy, uncomfortable terrain.

The King, too, did not consider hiking up to his lodge, preferring instead to be taken there the easy way by horse-drawn carriage. He particularly liked staying at his hunting lodge each year on his birthday.

The idea for a "hunting lodge with kitchens and stables" occurred to him in 1869. It was one of his less expensive projects, costing only 11,000 guilders in total, including the laying of a bridlepath from the valley. Just one year later the building was completed and in 1871 further extension work was carried out.

From the outside the lodge looks like a pleasant, modest dwelling: a pretty, two-floor mountain hut with wooden shutters and decoratively carved balcony railings. The raised ground floor, with bed chamber, study and dining room looks typically Alpine in style, but the first storey has an altogether different appearance. Here a "Moorish Hall", which the King had modelled on Turkish palaces, covers the entire interior space. A fountain plays in the centre of this splendid oriental hall, lavishly adorned with the finest carpets and gilded carvings, luxurious divans, soft pillows and richly upholstered benches, enamelled vases and ornate candelabras. In this setting, straight out of the pages of "A Thousand and One Nights", the King could indulge himself in fantasies as Caliph, Sultan, Sheikh, Emir and Lord of all the Orient.

Luise von Kobell, wife of the Cabinet Secretary, Eisenhart, reported in her memoires: "Here Ludwig II used to sit, attired in Turkish robes, reading, while his servants, dressed as Moslems, lounged around on carpets and cushions, smoking tobacco and sipping mocha, just as their royal master had ordered them to do; occasionally the King would look up, glance across to the stylish groups and smile imperiously. Incense burned in ornate bowls and huge fans of peacock feathers wafted the air, to heighten the oriental illusion."

The house on the Schachen was the first of Ludwig's oriental-style buildings. In 1876 the King obtained the Moorish Kiosk which had been designed for the World Exhibition in Paris in 1867, and placed it in the gardens of Linderhof Palace. Two years later, also for Linderhof, there followed a "Moroccan House", but this was sold to Oberammergau in 1886. Recently it was bought back by the castles' authorities and it is intended to restore it to its former splendour. In the Residence Palace in Munich the King had an Indian and oriental-style winter garden. A further "Moorish Hall" which he had planned for Neuschwanstein Castle never came to be built, nor did a Chinese Palace he had intended to have built near Lake Plansee in the Tyrol.

From today's perspective, the King's obsession with the Orient seems stranger than at the time it actually was. The picturesque splendour of foreign lands did not only fire Ludwig's imagination, the Orient was high fashion throughout the countries of Europe.

Ludwig's design for his Moorish Hall in the Schachen house was based on photographs. He himself had never been to the Orient – nor indeed to Capri – and had no intention of undertaking such journeys. Reality held little attraction for Ludwig, he preferred instead to create his own fantasy worlds in an environment which was familiar.

The "Moorish Hall" in the Hunting Lodge on the Schachen. This hall was Ludwig's first attempt at oriental-style architecture.

La « Salle Mauresque » du pavillon de chasse de Schachen; la première tentative architectonique de Louis en style oriental.

La «sala moresca» nel castello di caccia di Schachen, il primo tentativo di Ludwig di costruzione in stile orientale.

シャッヘン狩猟城の「ムーア風広間」。ルートヴィヒのオリエンタルスタイル建築の初の試みである。

Berg Castle

Splendid Isolation

"Berg Castle, in beautiful parkland near the lake, was the favourite seat of the late King Ludwig II; he prized its dreamy, isolated setting", we read in Amthor's "Führer durch das Bayerische Hochland" (Travellers' Guide to Upper Bavaria) published in 1894. "And indeed this most blessed monarch often returned from the fairytale splendour of his new palaces, Linderhof, Neuschwanstein and Herrenchiemsee, to the more modest apartments in this little castle; it was here that he had spent the most pleasant and enjoyable first years of his reign." – "Open daily except Sundays and June 13th. Entrance tickets (50 Pf.) can be obtained to the right of the entrance gates", we are informed. However, nowadays, the castle is lived in by a branch of the Wittelsbach family and is not open to the public. It cannot even be seen from the land; we can only catch a fleeting glimpse of it from the lake, while taking a boat trip.

Berg Castle is not a classic King Ludwig castle. The original structure was erected in the 17th century, later King Maximilian II had it adorned with Gothic battlements and corner turrets, and then Ludwig merely added one tower on the north side. In 1949, when listed building status was still a thing of the future, the Wittelsbachers had this tower torn down, together with all King Max's Gothic refinements, thus leaving just a plain, cube-shaped, rather unattractive country house.

If the visitor wants to visit Berg, all he or she can do is simply walk about one

Berg Castle, just 30 kilometres from the Residence Palace in Munich, was a favourite haunt of the King.

Le roi se plaisait à séjourner dans son château de Berg, à 30 kilomètres seulement de la résidence munichoise.

Il re si tratteneva volentieri nel suo castello di Berg, a soli 30 chilometri dalla Residenza di Monaco.

ミュンヘンのレジデンツから僅か30km離れたベルク城に王は滞在することを好んだ。

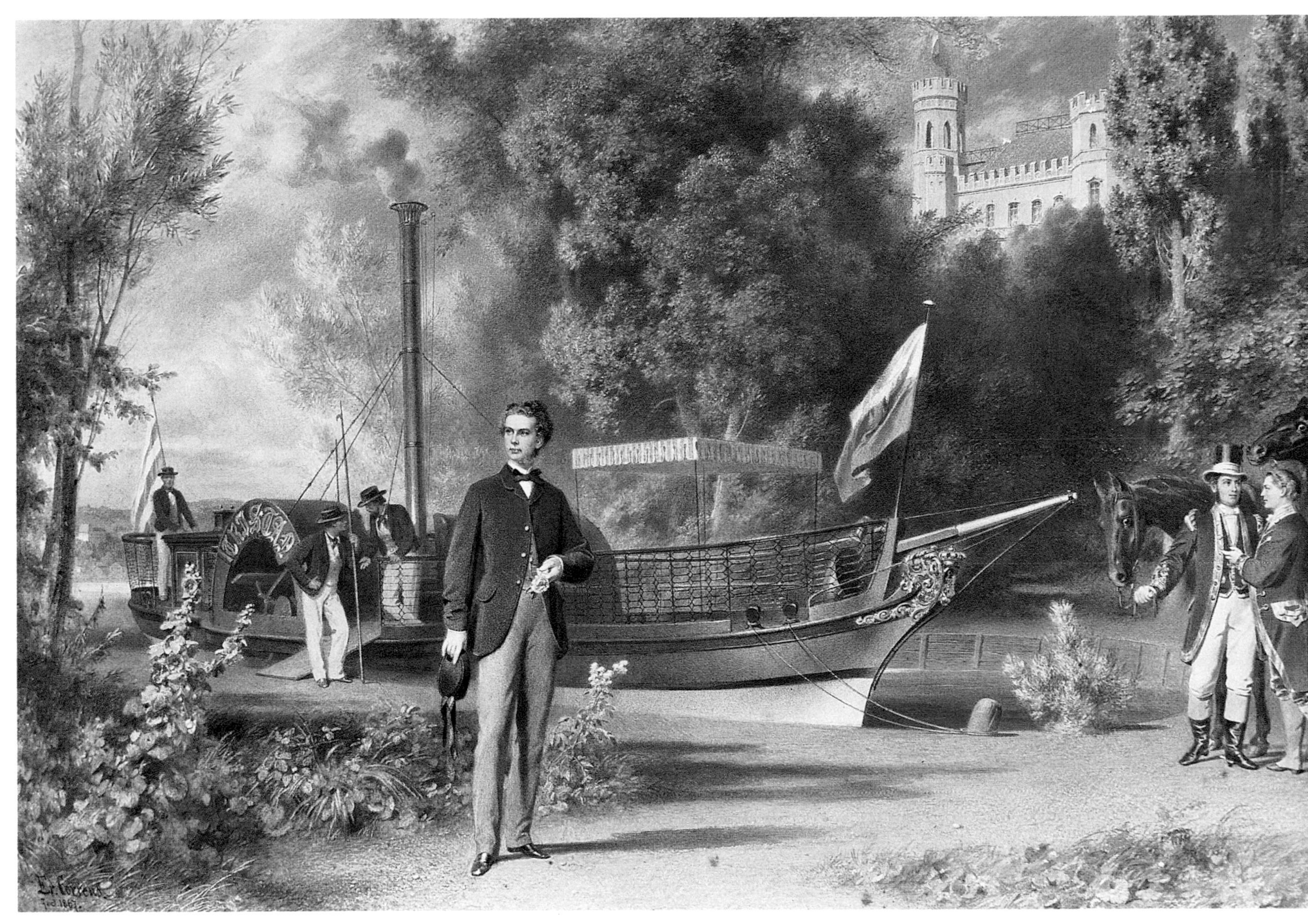

Ludwig, standing in front of his paddle-steamer "Tristan". The King often made the journey across to Roseninsel in this boat.

Louis sur son bateau à aubes « Tristan » sur lequel il aimait se rendre de Berg à Ile des Roses.

Ludwig davanti al suo piroscafo a ruote «Tristan» col quale amava recarsi da Berg alla Roseninsel.

外輪船「トリスタン」の前で。この船で王はベルクからローゼン島までを好んで航行した。

and a half kilometres around from the steamer jetty, along the edge of the private castle grounds, following the signs to the neo-Romanesque memorial chapel. The chapel, consecrated in 1900, and a neo-Gothic memorial column and a wooden cross in the lake are dedicated to the memory of King Ludwig; it was here, in 1886, at about the spot where the wooden cross stands wreathed with flowers, that he died.

Several benches have been placed here and a railing at the edge of the lake prevents visitors walking on the stony, reedy shore; a dented sign forbids the playing of games. Above the chapel another sign invites visitors to walk the "König-Ludwig-Weg" (King Ludwig Path) which leads from here all the way to Neuschwanstein "on paths, where the most famous Bavarian King often used to walk, ride or travel by coach." The walk, some 95 to 120 kilometres long, offers a choice of routes. And, as souvenir hunters like to steal the path markers, finding the one you want is not always an easy task. But wherever the walker strays, the scenery is always splendid.

Mounting Debts

DRASTIC MEASURES

The faithful castle tour guides never tire of pointing out that the King used no public funds for his castle projects, but instead used money from his own private income. This may be true in principle, but the reason lies in the fact that the Bavarian parliament simply refused to foot the royal bills.

The financial situation of the royal coffers steadily worsened after 1880. By 1884 the debts amounted to 7½ million marks. To cover this a bank loan was arranged, but just one year later the King's debts amounted to a further 6 million, and he was demanding as much again to be able to continue with his building plans. The King wrote to Feilitzsch, the Interior Minister, "If only that sum were provided which is necessary to cover the present debts, and no further monies were forthcoming for urgent building projects currently under construction, then this would not in the least serve my needs nor help the situation." The creditors were complaining more and more, malicious comments were appearing in the press and the Bavarian people just shook their heads in amazement. The King, however, remained unperturbed. He ordered his finance minister to "take the necessary steps to regulate the finances". The minister replied that it was impossible to find private sponsors, and that funds from the national budget could only be granted by

Design for a fantastic royal barge.

Ebauche pour une barque somptueuse destinée au roi.

Schizzo di una lussuosa barca.

王のためのキームゼー装飾舟バークのスケッチ。

Ludwig's plan to build Falkenstein Castle was not carried out.

Le projet de Louis de construire le château Falkenstein n'a jamais été réalisé.

Il progetto di Ludwig di costruire il castello di Falkenstein non fu realizzato.

ルートヴィヒによるプフロンテン近郊のラウプリッター・ファルケンシュタイン城の計画は資金上の問題から現実化されることはなかった。

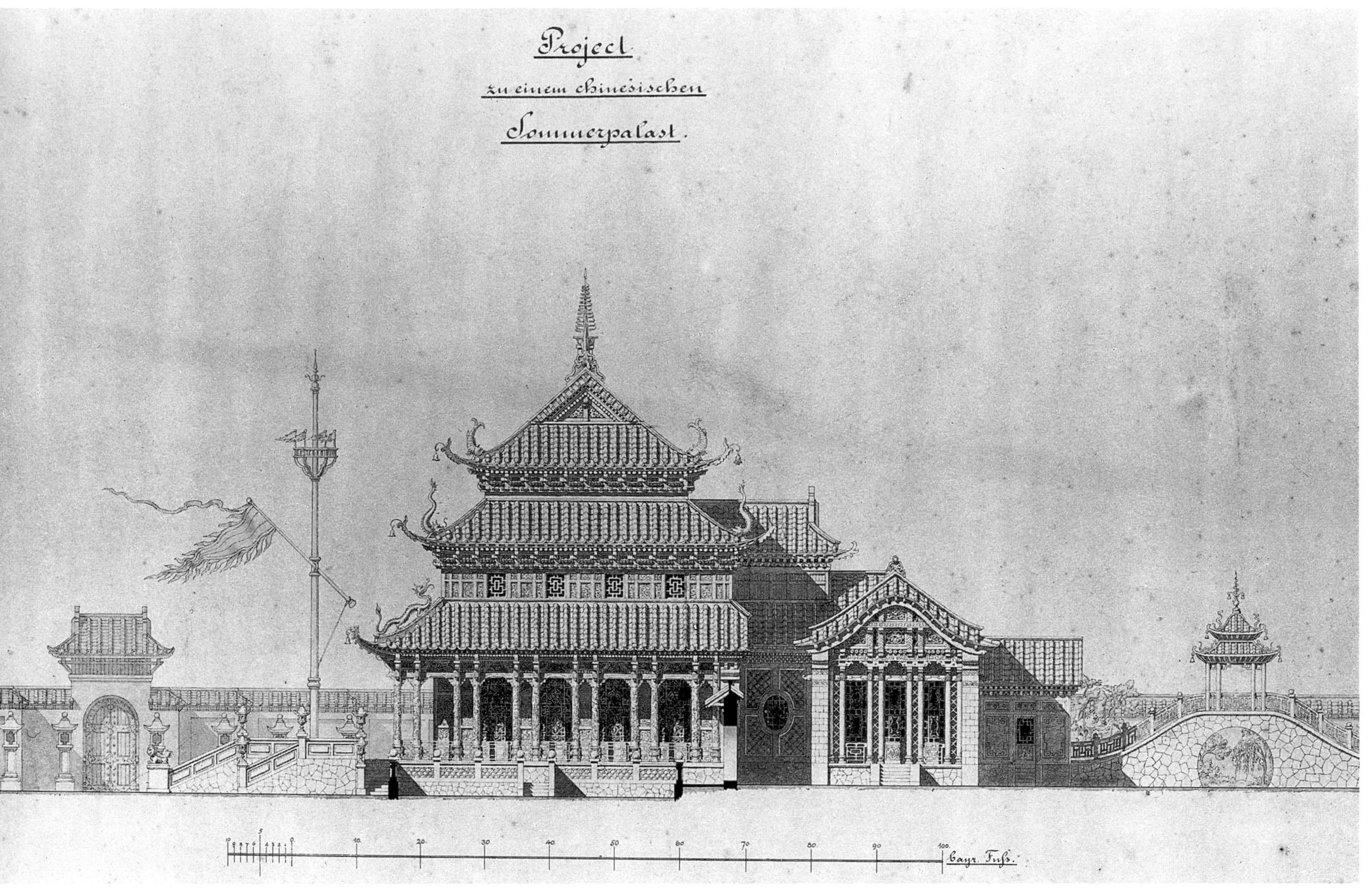

The King's last design: a Chinese palace.

Le dernier projet du roi: un palais chinois.

L'ultimo progetto del re: un palazzo in stile cinese.

王の最後の構想： 中国風宮殿

the state parliament, something which it was extremely unlikely to do; moreover, if he, the minister, were to enter into such consultations with parliament, it would lead to highly embarassing discussions which would damage the reputation of the monarchy. Furthermore, the minister feared, impatient creditors were about to start proceedings to impound the castles. The only solution was to stop all further building work and to save money. This option, however, was furthest from the King's mind.

The King then decided to take matters into his own hands and teach the incapable minister a lesson; he sent adjutants and confidants around the world to take out loans, and he engaged various daring young men to travel to Frankfurt, Paris, Berlin and Stuttgart and break into the Rothschild bank offices there and bring back the necessary millions to their King. These last envoys turned out to be fraudulent rogues, who simply had a good time in the big cities and never even attempted to carry out any bank robbery, returning instead with tall tales of how they had almost pulled it off, only to be foiled at the last minute. What a shame! If they had done their duty, perhaps we would now have one or two more, lucrative King Ludwig castles.

Deposed!

AND ESCORTED FROM YOUR CASTLE

It had been known for some time that the King was suffering from more than just mild delusions. The King was ill – probably a weakness from the mother's side (of course, there was nothing wrong with the Bavarian Wittelsbachers); hers was a rather suspect lineage and now Ludwig and his brother, Otto, who had been mentally deranged for 10 years, shared in these Hohenzollern genetic defects.

As long as the royal eccentricities remained harmless, and were still conducive to influence by the Cabinet, then the situation was tolerable. But what was to be done with a King who was bringing shame upon his entire country, becoming more and more of a burden, and damaging the reputation of the state, the monarchy and finally also undermining the position of his ministers?

The answer was to rid oneself of him. To certify him unfit to govern and to depose him.

According to the terms of the constitution, an official report was necessary in order to be able to do this; the report had to state that the King "is prevented from exercising government by some cause which persists in its effects for a period of more than one year". The report was made. Professor Bernhard Gudden, the most well known German psychiatrist at the time, and three other doctors, confirmed on June 8th, 1886:

"His Majesty is in an advanced stage of

The King on his last journey, being escorted as a prisoner from Neuschwanstein to Berg.

Le roi lors de son dernier voyage qui le mène en tant que prisonnier de Neuschwanstein au château de Berg.

Il re nel suo ultimo viaggio che lo conduce da Neuschwanstein al castello di Berg in veste di prigioniero.

mental illness, and that illness takes the form of the disease known to all doctors for the insane as paranoia. The gradual and inevitable progress of this disease has already been affecting His Majesty for quite a long time, over a number of years, to the extent that he is now to be considered incurable. A further decline of His Majesty's mental capacities will most certainly occur."

One rather worrying aspect of this report is that it is only based on the accounts of witnesses; no actual examination of the King ever took place, but it seems highly unlikely that the King would in any case have consented to such an examination.

On June 9th the King was certified unfit to govern; the next day, June 10th, his uncle, Prince Luitpold took over the government and at four o'clock in the morning a state commission arrived at Neuschwanstein to inform the King.

An anonymous demand for the King's abdication – a move which the King himself had often considered.

Des calomnieurs anonymes exigèrent l'abdication du roi – lui-même y avait souvent songé.

Anonimi detrattori chiesero l'allontanamento dal trono del re che, del resto, egli stesso aveva preso in considerazione in ripetute occasioni.

匿名の中傷が王の退位を強要した。王はすでに自分でもしばしば退位を考えていた。

Their mission was, however, not successful. The commission was turned away at the castle gates and then proceeded to try and force its way in. An old baroness and the police chased them away, and the gentlemen of the commission retired to Hohenschwangau Castle to reconsider. There the King sent his gendarmes to arrest them, bring them back to Neuschwanstein and lock them up. The King then ordered that the commissioners should have their eyes gouged out and that they should be skinned; the chief guard did not obey this command, because, as he said, he knew, "that punishments can only be carried out on the orders of a judge".

After a few hours the men of the commission were set free and they returned to Munich. On June 12th new commissioners arrived at the castle, and these were more successful in delivering their message.

"Aha!", was the King's response to their news, "So Prince Luitpold has finally managed it. But he need not have used all that cunning – if only he had said, then I would have renounced my governmental obligations and gone abroad."

At four o'clock in the morning of the twelfth of June the commission set off from Neuschwanstein, with the King, for Berg Castle. There they arrived at 12 o'clock after an uneventful journey. An announcement in the "Allgemeine Zeitung" stated: "Accompanying the King were Dr Gudden and Dr Müller, an assistant doctor, also several attendants and guards. The King's appearance has not changed; he stands erect and his behaviour is calm. The King is most gracious in his dealings with Dr Gudden and he shall for the time being be remaining here."

For the time being.

The bed chamber of the King in Neuschwanstein. Here the psychiatrists informed him that he had been deposed.

La chambre à coucher du roi à Neuschwanstein. C'est ici que la commission des psychiatres lui communiqua sa destitution.

La camera da letto del re a Neuschwanstein. Qui il consulto degli psichiatri gli comunicò la sua deposizione.

ノイシュヴァンシュタインの王の寝室。ここで精神病医委員会は王の解任を彼に伝えた。

The Tragic End

TREACHERY AND MURDER

On Whit Sunday, June 13th, 1886, the King died, aged 40 years, nine months, two weeks and five days. He drowned in Lake Starnberg, 966 paces away from Berg Castle. Did he really drown? Why? How? What on earth was he doing in the ice-cold waters of the lake on a Sunday evening in his coat and hat, carrying an umbrella?

It was raining and rather cool. Nevertheless the King and his psychiatrist Dr Bernhard Gudden had set out on an evening walk through the castle grounds. They left the castle at 18.45 pm. A guard who had been following them at a discrete distance was sent back by Dr Gudden. The King had apparently resigned himself to his fate and was quite calm and easy to handle, and so precautionary measures seemed unnecessary, and in any case there were a number of gendarmes about in the grounds.

They were expected back at half past seven, but they didn't come. A quarter to eight and still no King, no psychiatrist; eight o'clock – still no sign of them. Where were they then? It had started to rain more heavily, perhaps they had sought shelter somewhere? People in the castle became very nervous, search parties spread out, attendants, guards, doctors, policemen and courtiers all searched through the grounds carrying lanterns and torches.

Nine o'clock came, then half past, and still no sign of them. At last, at ten o'clock Georg Ritter, one of the court servants, spotted "something black quite near to the banks", pulled it out of the water, and recognised it as "the frock-coat of His Majesty, it being impossible to mistake in view of its size and weight". Then the umbrella and the hat came into view, then Gudden's hat, and about eleven o'clock the castle administrator Huber discovered the bodies of the dead King and his doctor. Huber reported:

King Ludwig was dead, but for his faithful, wild mountain people he still lived on.

Le roi Louis était mort, mais pour son peuple de montagne fidèle et sauvage, il vit encore.

Re Ludwig era morto, ma continuò a vivere per il suo fidato e rude popolo montanaro.

ルートヴィヒ王は死んだが、彼の忠実で粗野な山の民にとっては生き続けた。

"When Dr Müller and I found the bodies, they were floating about twenty to twenty-five paces out from the edge of the lake, one behind the other, first the body of His Majesty, and then the other body about a table's length behind. Both were floating face down. I jumped from the boat I was in into the water, which reached up to my chest, and I took hold of both bodies and pushed them towards the shore. There others who had gathered on the banks helped me to take them out of the water and place them in the boat. Dr Gudden's body was fully clothed, His Majesty was in his shirt sleeves."

Apart from a few grazes on the knees,

When Dr Gudden set off with the King for an evening walk, he sent the guard back to the castle.

Avant d'entreprendre sa promenade du soir avec le roi, le Docteur Gudden renvoie le gardien.

Quando il Dottor Gudden si avviò alla passeggiata serale col re, egli rimandò il guardiano al castello.

グッデン医師は王と夜の散歩に出かける時には監視人を城に返した。

the King had no injuries. Dr Gudden had scratches on the forehead and the nose, and a black eye. The King's pocket watch had stopped at 18.54 pm. Gudden's assistant doctor, Dr Müller, recalled: "The expression on the face of the King was sinister, domineering, almost tyrannical, and Gudden's face still bore that same friendly smile that was so familar to his many patients."

What had happened? There were no witnesses, no-one had heard anything, and the official protocol did not give any cause of death. And so everyone can make up their own mind on what really took place.

The popular version is that Ludwig and Dr Gudden drowned. However, the guide on our tour of Herrenchiemsee Palace sows seeds of doubt about this: "On June 13th the King had to, in other words he

The King's personal physician, Dr Gudden, fighting with his patient.

Le Docteur Gudden, médecin attitré, en lutte avec le roi.

Il medico personale, Dottor Gudden, mentre lotta con il re.

王と争う侍医グッデン。

At eleven o'clock at night the bodies were recovered.

Onze heures du soir: les cadavres sont repêchés.

Di notte alle undici: vengono scoperti i corpi.

夜11時： 遺体が収容された。

A wooden cross in Lake Starnberg marks the spot where Ludwig drowned.

La croix du Lac de Starnberg indique: c'est ici que se noya le roi.

La croce del lago Starnberg dice: qui è annegato Ludwig.

シュタルベルガー湖の十字架が示す：
この地にてルートヴィヒ溺死。

Admirers of King Ludwig always ensure that fresh flowers adorn the picture of the King in the Memorial Chapel in Berg.

Les admirateurs de Louis II n'oublient jamais de déposer des fleurs devant le portrait du roi dans la chapelle commémorative de Berg.

Ludwig II: gli ammiratori non scordano di ornare di fiori l'immagine del re nella cappella commemorativa di Berg.

ルートヴィヒ　世の敬慕者はベルク城の記念礼拝堂にある王の肖像に花を飾るのを欠かさない。

was forced to, take a walk with his personal physician Dr Gudden, and both drowned in Lake Starnberg. But three things point to it not being a normal drowning. Firstly they were both drowned. Secondly the King was a very good swimmer, and thirdly the part of the lake in which they drowned was not in the least deep. But unfortunately, we have no proof of how the King actually did die. It is a mystery and will remain so because the Wittelsbachers, who most probably know what actually happened, will never say."

They, the Wittelsbachers, the descendants of the Bavarian royal family, are keeping their secret family archives firmly closed and in doing so they open the way for all manner of speculation.

The suicide theory is very widespread: the King, deposed, declared unfit and mentally ill, locked in his castle, full of despair, decides to kill himself. He had in fact often enough said that he would "think about killing himself", if his "main pleasure in life", building, were to be taken away from him.

According to this theory, about ten minutes into their walk, the King runs away from the doctor. Gudden follows him, trying to hold him back. He catches

The Memorial Chapel to the King, built 1896–1900 in the early Romanesque style, in the grounds of Berg Castle.

La chapelle commémorative vouée au roi dans le parc du château de Berg; une construction centrale en nouveau style roman précoce, construite entre 1896 et 1900.

La cappella commemorativa del re nel parco del castello di Berg, una nuova costruzione centrale in stile preromanico sorsero dal 1896 al 1900.

ベルク城の庭園の王記念礼拝堂。新初期ロマン派の集中建築。
1896–1900年に建造された。

him by the collar, but the King deftly slips out of his frock-coat, and hurries on. Gudden thinks: If I get back on my own without the King there will be hell to pay, so he catches up with the King again, and a struggle starts – the large, heavy (almost two and a half hundredweight) King hits Gudden, overcomes him, strangles him and dumps him in the lake. Gudden drowns. Ludwig wades further out into the lake, lowers his head resignedly into the waters and, with an iron will, holds it down until he also drowns.

This all sounds rather unlikely and most probably not even physically possible, because you would think that one's head would automatically come back up to the surface in such a case. Thus the heart-attack theory is the more believable: the King suffers a heart attack after his strenuous efforts in the struggle with Dr Gudden. This version of the tale has the added attraction that the King would no longer be affected by the stigma of having committed suicide.

If we assume that Dr Gudden also suffered a heart attack – he was after all 62 years old and used neither to fist fights, nor bathing fully clothed in water at a mere 12°C – then the King would also not

The King's sarcophagus in the Church of Saint Michael in Munich. Candles are lit in memory of the king.

Le sarcophage du roi dans l'église Saint Michael à Munich. Son peuple allume des cierges en son honneur.

Il sarcofago del re nella Chiesa di San Michele a Monaco. Il suo popolo vi accende candele.

ミュンヘンにある聖ミヒャエル教会の王の石棺。人々は蝋燭を灯す。

The Bavarian people can pay their respects to King Ludwig in the Residence Chapel in Munich.

Le peuple peut prendre congé de son roi dans l'ancienne chapelle de la Résidence à Munich.

Nella vecchia cappella della residenza di Monaco il popolo può congedarsi dal suo re.

ミュンヘンの旧レジデンツで人々は王に別れを告げることを許される。

be guilty of manslaughter; this would be an altogether more satisfactory variant.

The King Ludwig supporters tend towards the belief that the King had no intention of committing suicide, because if he had wanted to, he would have had plenty of opportunity to do so in Neuschwanstein. For them the words of one of the King Ludwig songs hold true:

> *"Der König wollt' schwimmen über den See zu den Tausenden seiner Getreuen."*
>
> *"The King wanted to swim across the lake, where thousands of his faithful friends did wait."*

He was trying to escape (which, incidentally, would also have been much easier to do from Neuschwanstein).

The proof for their theory is in the fresh wheel marks which were found in front of the castle gates. This shows that a coach had been waiting here; the King was aiming to swim around to it, because the castle gates were locked. In any case many boats had been spotted out on the lake, rowed there by brave fishermen sent by the Empress Elisabeth. This theory, too, concludes with the King suffering a heart attack.

If this version is true, one can only say that the organisation of the escape plan could hardly have been worse. It was obvious that Gudden would not just stand by and watch, and clearly it would have been just as easy for the King's helpers to

After Ludwig's death the crown passed to his mentally ill brother, Otto. Prince Luitpold, Otto's uncle, ruled for him as Prince Regent. Here he is seen is his favourite pose as a hunter.

Après la mort de Louis, la couronne est passée à son frère Otto, qui souffrait d'une maladie mentale. Son oncle, Prince Luitpold, assura alors la régence à sa place. Il est ici présenté dans sa pose préférée en costume de chasseur.

Dopo la morte di Ludwig la corona passò a suo fratello Otto, psichicamente infermo. Il principe Luitpold, suo zio, fu reggente per lui, lo vediamo qui nella sua posa preferita die cacciatore.

ルートヴィヒの死後、王位は精神病を患っていた弟オットーに移った。
その代わりに叔父のルイトポルド公が摂生を取った。
この絵は彼の好んだ狩猟者のポーズである。

collect him from the banks, than for the King to have to jump into the water.

There were supposed to have been many traces of the struggle between Ludwig and his psychiatrist in the reeds and at the water's edge, but were they really there? And if these traces were there, were they real? Or perhaps they could have been false traces someone had made in order to confuse and mislead the people and the clerks writing up the evidence? And if so, then who?

Maybe it could have been like this: the King, who had had a heavy meal before the walk, was secretly administered chloroform, so that he stumbled, dazed and bemused, to the edge of the lake, and then Gudden only needed to give a slight push to topple him into the water. But the King was too near the banks, so the treacherous doctor grabbed hold of him again and pulled him out further into the lake. The King then came to, struggled with Gudden, shouting, "You scoundrel, you'll drown for this!", and then fell back again overcome once more by the chloroform, and drowned.

Why, then, would Gudden wish to kill the King? Who had put him up to it? Were they perhaps rivals and conspirators within the Wittelsbach family? Or a despicable band of ministers? Or, as the Bavarian people long suspected, was it the Prussians? – "Dr Gudden in cahoots

A popular souvenir in the years following the King's death: King Ludwig postcards singing the King's praises in verse.

Les hit-parades des ventes de l'époque: les cartes postales du roi Louis décorées de vers exprimant louanges, gloire et fidélité.

Must d'epoca: cartoline del Re Ludwig, ornate di versetti di lode, di gloria e di fedeltà.

当時のベストセラー： ルートヴィヒ王の絵葉書。賞賛と賛美、忠誠の詩句に飾られている。

with Bismarck, the man known as the false chancellor"?

Another theory claims that the King was probably shot, and that two bullet holes were supposed to have been found in the King's jacket – now, sadly, lost. These murderous shots came from court or ministerial circles, or perhaps the Prussians, possibly even the anarchists.

Or maybe the shot came from a police weapon. This was how it happened, according to a letter to the "Süddeutsche Zeitung" in 1979: the King fled into the water, Gudden set off after him and the two entered into a fight. A policeman, watching the struggle, "sees that things are going badly for Dr Gudden, and aims two shots at the King, probably so as to rescue Dr Gudden. The shots hit the King in the back. One can imagine that the King's devoted subjects would have had some difficulty in accepting this explanation. So, after an appropriate delay, an announcement was made to the people that the King had died in a mysterious accident. By the time the King was laid out in state, there was no sign of the gunshot wounds. The unfortunate police officer

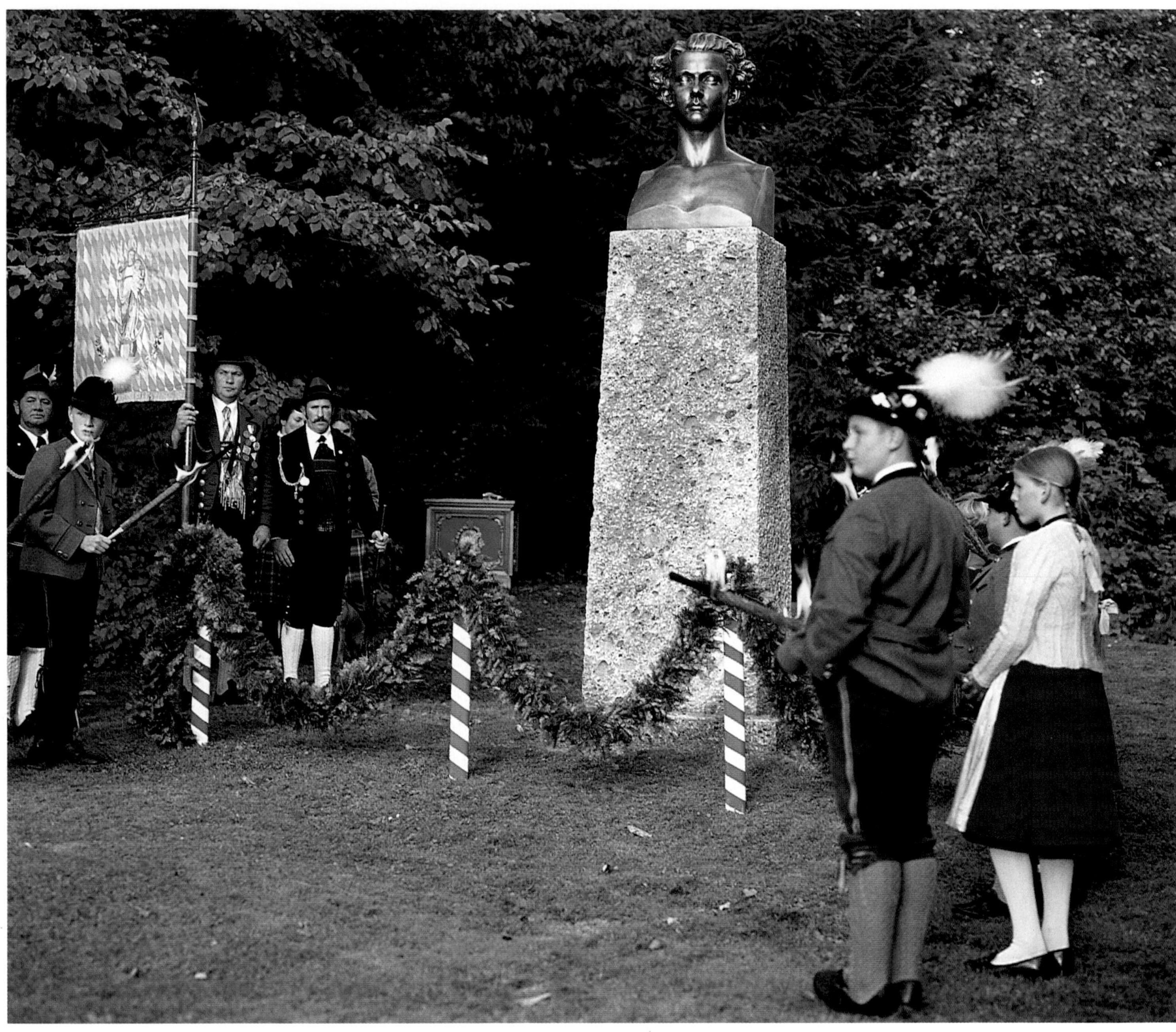

was sworn to silence and sent for his punishment to serve in the northernmost regions of Bavaria – in Lower Franconia."

The romantics among the Ludwig faithfuls tell another story: the King did not die, nor was he shot, nor even did he die of a heart attack. Rescuers escaped with him after Gudden's death. The body that was found in the lake, laid in state and finally buried in the sarcophagus was in fact a wax effigy of the King.

Ludwig himself lived on, happily and quite contentedly in Lower Bavaria or somewhere in the wilds of the Balkans. Would this not be the nicest, happiest, and most satisfactory ending to a tragic story? It may not be the most probable of the various versions, but certainly the most appropriate one for a storybook King.

Ludwig Memorial in Linderhof, unveiled in 1982.

Le monument à la mémoire de Louis à Linderhof, dévoilé en 1982.

Il monumento di Ludwig a Linderhof, scoperto nel 1982.

リンダーホーフのルートヴィヒ記念碑。1982年に除幕。

Schrobenhausen
Donau
Landshut
Günzburg
Augsburg
Freising
Eggenfelden
Erdinger Moos
Rottal
Erding
Simbach
Königsbrunn
Dachau
Dorfen
Waldkraiburg
Altötting
Fürstenfeld-
bruck
MÜNCHEN
Ebersberg
Mindelheim
Landsberg
Herrsching
Ammer-
see
Andechs
Starnberg
Isar
Wasser-
burg
Memmingen
Inn
Dießen
Lech
Possenhofen
Berg
Chiemgau
Tutzing
Wolfratshausen
Chiemsee
Traunstein
Laufen
Kaufbeuren
Starnberger
See
Herrenchiemsee
Rosenheim
Pfaffenwinkel
Weilheim
Schongau
Bad Tölz
Miesbach
Bad
Reichenhall
Tegernsee
Tegernsee
Brannenburg
Rottenbuch
Wies
Staffelsee
Reit im
Winkl
Murnau
Ammer
Berchtesgaden
ALLGÄU
Forggensee
Oberammergau
Walchen-
see
Pfronten
Linderhof
Watzmann
2713
Königs-
see
Neuschwanstein
Hohenschwangau
Ettal
Füssen
Werdenfelser Land
Sonthofen
Zugspitze
2962
Garmisch-
Partenkirchen
Mittenwald
Schachen

Acknowledgements

The publishers would like to acknowledge the following for their help in supplying illustrative material and for giving their permission to reproduce it. (This list includes additional information on the illustrations and details of locations.)

Bayerische Verwaltung der staatlichen Schlösser, Gärten und Seen, Munich: p. 17 (lithograph by J. Woelffle of a drawing by Erich Correns; Herrenchiemsee, Ludwig II Museum), p. 20 (coloured photograph based on a watercolour by Ernst Rietschel, 1850; Herrenchiemsee, Ludwig II Museum), p. 24 (Bavarian royal insignia by Martin Guillaume Biennais, Paris 1906; Munich, Residence Palace, Treasury), p. 25 and title motif ("King Ludwig II in Bavarian general's uniform and coronation robe", painting by Ferdinand Piloty, 1865; Herrenchiemsee, Ludwig II Museum), p. 38/39 (Design elevation of Neuschwanstein Castle from the northeast, gouache by Christian Jank, 1869; Herrenchiemsee, Ludwig II Museum, WAF), p. 62, p. 75, p. 77 (King Ludwig II as "Grand Master of the Order of the Knights of Saint George", painting by Gabriel Schachinger, 1887; Herrenchiemsee, Ludwig II Museum), p. 93 ("King Ludwig II, and his paddle-steamer 'Tristan', coming ashore at Berg Castle", a watercolour by Erich Correns, 1867; Herrenchiemsee, Ludwig II Museum), p. 94 (Design for a fantastic royal barge, gouache by Franz Seitz, ca. 1870; Herrenchiemsee, Ludwig II Museum), p. 95 (First design for Falkenstein Castle, gouache by Christian Jank, 1883; Herrenchiemsee, Ludwig II Museum), p. 96 (Design for a project for a Chinese summer palace (elevation) by Julius Hofmann, 1886; Herrenchiemsee, Ludwig II Museum).
Robert Bechteler, Sonthofen: p. 66/67
Bildarchiv Bruckmann, Munich: p. 1 (photograph by Franz Hanfstaengl, 1879), p. 34, bottom, p. 36, p. 37, top (photograph by Joseph Albert, 1867), p. 40 (photograph by Franz Hanfstaengl, 1867), p. 42, top, p. 55 (photograph by Franz Hanfstaengl), p. 97, p. 98
Bildarchiv Huber, Garmisch-Partenkirchen: p. 4/5, p. 10/11 (R. Schmid), p. 26/27 (B. Radelt), p. 34, top, p. 85 (R. Schmid), p. 87
Sammlung Jean Louis, Munich: p. 13, p. 15, left, p. 15, right, p. 21, top, p. 21, bottom right, p. 29 (lithograph), p. 30 (wood engraving of a drawing by Joseph Watter in "Über Land und Meer", 1872), p. 31, p. 41, p. 42, bottom (watercolour probably by Gottfried Semper, 1867; Photo: Bayreuth, Nationalarchiv der Richard-Wagner-Stiftung/Richard-Wagner-Gedenkstätte), p. 48 (wood engraving of a drawing by Robert Assmus in the "Gartenlaube", 1886), p. 84 (wood engraving of a drawing by W. Grögler in the "Leipziger Illustrirte Zeitung" of 13.08.1887), p. 88 (wood engraving of a design by Gustav Sundblad in the "Gartenlaube", ca. 1880), p. 100 (representation on the occasion of the unveiling of the memorial monument to King Ludwig II in Murnau on August 26th, 1894), p. 107 (wood engraving of a drawing by H. Albrecht in the "Gartenlaube", 1886), p. 109, left, p. 109, right
Joachim Kankel, Munich: p. 44
Luftbild Klammet & Aberl, Ohlstadt: p. 78/79 (permission granted by the Government of Upper Bavaria, no. G43/1125)
Wolfgang Lauter, Munich: p. 18/19
MAURITIUS: p. 6/7 (Nägele), p. 32/33 (Kabes), inside back cover (Pigneter)
Richard Mayer, Munich: Inside front cover, p. 2/3, p. 8/9, p. 12, p. 23, p. 49, p. 51, p. 52, p. 53, p. 54, p. 56, top, p. 57, p. 58, p. 59, p. 61, p. 63, p. 69, p. 70, p. 71, p. 73, p. 74, p. 81, p. 82/83, p. 86, p. 89, p. 91, p. 103, p. 104, p. 105, p. 106, cover motifs: Neuschwanstein, Linderhof, Herrenchiemsee
Ludwig Merkle, Munich: p. 80
Werner Neumeister, Munich: p. 22, p. 43 ("King Ludwig II and Richard Wagner", gouache by Fritz Bergen), p. 46/47 ("Ludwig II on a night-time sleigh ride from Neuschwanstein to Linderhof", oil painting by R. Wenig; Munich, Marstallmuseum in Nymphenburg Palace, Bayerische Verwaltung der staatlichen Schlösser, Gärten und Seen), p. 50 ("Ludwig II on the balcony of the Throne Room in Neuschwanstein", oil painting by Ferdinand Leeke), p. 60, p. 64, p. 65, p. 76, p. 99, p. 110
Alexander Rauch, Munich: p. 72
Extracted from: Anton Sailer, Bayerns Märchenkönig, 4th ed. 1992, Bruckmann, Munich: p. 14, top, p. 14, bottom, p. 21, bottom left, p. 28, p. 37, bottom, p. 45, top, p. 45, bottom, p. 56, bottom, p. 92, p. 101, p. 102, top, p. 102, bottom, p. 108 ("Prince Regent Luitpold as a hunter", painting by Franz von Defregger, 1880)
Wittelsbacher Ausgleichsfonds, Munich: p. 35 ("Empress Elisabeth of Austria", oil painting by Franz Schrotzberg)